THE AMERICAN NIGHTMARE
How Inflation, Debt, and Banks Hijacked the American Dream

Paperback ISBN: 979-8-9957752-0-1
eBook ISBN: 979-8-9957752-1-8

The information provided in this book is designed to provide helpful information on the subjects discussed. The author's books are only meant to provide the reader with the basic knowledge of certain topics without any guarantees concerning results. This book is for educational and entertainment purposes only. While most care has been taken in compiling the information contained in this book, no responsibility can be accepted by the author for any errors or omissions that may be made. Neither can any liability be accepted by the publisher for any damages, losses, or costs resulting from using the information contained within these pages.

THE AMERICAN DREAM NIGHTMARE

HOW INFLATION, DEBT, AND BANKS HIJACKED THE AMERICAN DREAM

John Vasquez

DEDICATION

This book is dedicated to my family, my foundation, my strength, and my reason. To my children, you are my legacy, my greatest responsibility, and my deepest source of purpose. Every lesson, every sacrifice, and every battle I have fought was with you in mind. May this work serve as a guide long after I am gone so you walk with strength, think with clarity, and lead with honor. To my family who stood beside me through the storms, through the uncertainty, the setbacks, and the climb, you never wavered. You believed when belief was hard and held the line when I was still learning how. This is as much yours as it is mine. To the thousands of Warriors across the world who chose discipline over comfort, truth over illusion, and action over excuses, you are the ripple, you are the shift, and you are the ones who broke the cycle so your bloodline could rise. We are not victims of circumstance, we are builders of legacy. We rise, we fight, and we never back down.

CONTENTS

INTRODUCTION

YOU DIDN'T FAIL. THE SYSTEM DID.

My name is John Vasquez, though many people know me as Coach JV.

For the past eight years, after leaving the banking system, I have spent an extraordinary amount of time studying how money actually works. Not the simplified version taught in school textbooks. Not the reassuring explanations offered in political speeches or financial television. I mean the underlying structure itself - how money is created, how banking functions, how inflation moves through an economy, and how debt quietly shapes the lives of millions of people.

This journey began with a simple observation. Something about the financial world no longer made sense. Many people feel this instinctively, even if they struggle to explain it. They work harder than previous generations seemed to need to. They earn more degrees, carry more responsibility, and spend more years building careers. Yet the outcomes often feel smaller and more fragile.

- Homes appear further out of reach.
- Savings grow slowly while costs rise quickly.
- Retirement feels uncertain even after decades of work.

For many people, the natural conclusion is personal failure. They assume they made the wrong decisions, chose the wrong career, or simply did not work hard enough. The narrative becomes deeply personal because the system surrounding them remains invisible.

But when the structure becomes visible, the story changes.

Consider a simple comparison. Your grandparents could often buy a home, raise children, and retire on a single income. For many families today, two full-time incomes struggle to produce the same level of stability. The difference is often explained away as cultural change or personal discipline.

The data tells a different story.

According to research from the U.S. Bureau of Labor Statistics and the Federal Reserve Bank of St. Louis, the U.S. dollar has lost roughly 96 to 97 percent of its purchasing power since 1913. What one dollar could buy a century ago now requires nearly thirty dollars.

The effort required to earn money has not increased thirty times. The value of the money itself has changed. This shift helps explain why so many people feel as though they are running faster simply to remain in the same place. The problem is not always effort. Sometimes the problem is the unit of measurement.

Over time, this quiet erosion reshapes entire societies.

The American Dream, once defined by home ownership and financial stability, has gradually become harder to reach for many families. Homeownership rates have declined in several areas while institutional investors purchase residential properties at increasing scale. At the same time, household debt continues rising as families borrow simply to maintain living standards that previous generations achieved with income alone.

These patterns exist alongside a national debt that continues expanding. As of this writing, U.S. federal debt has surpassed $38 trillion according to Treasury data. Credit card debt has exceeded $1 trillion, a level the Federal Reserve recently described as a historic high. The nation's debt-to-GDP ratio now exceeds 120 percent, meaning the country owes more than it produces in an entire year.

Numbers like these are often discussed in political debates, yet their deeper meaning rarely reaches ordinary households.

Debt at this scale eventually influences everything. It shapes interest rates, housing affordability, wages, and the purchasing power of the currency itself. When governments rely heavily on borrowing, the monetary system gradually adjusts in ways that reduce the real value of money over time.

Most people feel the consequences long before they understand the mechanism. They see prices rising faster than salaries. They notice that everyday expenses consume larger portions of income. They discover that saving money in traditional accounts produces very little growth while the cost of living continues climbing. The experience feels confusing because the system itself is rarely explained clearly.

Every election cycle promises relief. Political campaigns promise to strengthen the middle class, stabilize the economy, and restore prosperity to working families. Yet across decades the same pattern continues appearing.

Debt increases.
Costs rise.
Households work longer hours to maintain the same standard of living.

The result is a quiet trade that many people never consciously agreed to. To earn more money, people must give up more time.

This dynamic extends beyond economics. It reshapes family life as well. Millions of households now depend on two full-time incomes simply to cover housing, healthcare, education, and transportation. Parents work longer hours while children spend more time in institutional care.

Over time, the pressure becomes normalized.

People begin assuming this is simply how modern life works. And when stability remains difficult to achieve, many people turn the blame inward. They believe they made mistakes. They believe they lacked discipline. They believe something about their own decisions must explain the outcome.

Yet when the system itself becomes visible, a different explanation appears.

Many people were simply never taught how the system operates. For the past several years, our team has coached more than fourteen thousand individuals across the world through financial education programs designed to address this exact gap. The pattern we observe repeatedly is not laziness or lack of effort. It is a lack of structural understanding.

From a very early age, most people are trained to follow a particular financial script.

- Study hard.
- Get a job.
- Trade time for money.
- Spend what you need.
- Save what remains.

Savings are typically placed in banks that pay minimal interest while using those deposits to generate far greater profits through lending and investment activity. At the same time, the currency stored in those accounts gradually loses purchasing power through inflation. Inflation functions like a silent tax. It reduces the value of money slowly enough that many people never notice the full effect. Wage earners and savers tend to feel its impact most strongly, while individuals who own appreciating assets often benefit from the same system.

None of this happens by accident.

The education system, banking system, and corporate structure developed in ways that reinforced this model. If you grew up in a middle-class or working-class household and attended public school, the structure surrounding you likely encouraged the same financial habits.

Over time those habits become programming. And programming is a powerful word because it explains how financial behavior often travels across generations. Wealthy families tend to pass down systems, knowledge, and confidence about money. Families without that knowledge often pass down caution and fear.

You have probably heard some of these phrases before.

- Money does not grow on trees.
- We cannot afford that.
- Investing is risky.

These ideas may have been shared with good intentions, yet they quietly shape how people think about opportunity and ownership. Over time belief becomes identity, and identity influences behavior. This pattern helps explain why wealth remains concentrated across generations. It is rarely about intelligence alone. It is usually about access to knowledge and systems that allow families to understand how money actually functions.

The truth is that these patterns can change. Every family history contains a moment when someone decides to learn what previous generations never had the chance to study. One person begins examining the system rather than assuming it will always work the same way it once did.

That individual becomes the generational shifter.

This book exists for that person. In the chapters ahead, we will explore how the modern debt-based monetary system was constructed, how money is created through banking, how inflation gradually erodes purchasing power, and why interest quietly transfers wealth across generations. You will also learn why certain individuals and institutions consistently benefit from economic cycles while others struggle to keep pace.

This is not a book about getting rich quickly. It is a book about understanding the structure you live inside. Because once the system becomes visible, a different path begins to emerge. A path built on financial literacy, discipline, ownership, and long-term thinking. Somewhere in every family tree, one person chooses to see the system clearly and build a different future.

Perhaps that person is **you**.

CHAPTER 1

THE DREAM THEY SOLD US

The Middle Class Was Designed

Before the middle class had a name, before it had a shape or a promise attached to it, wealth lived close to the body. It lived where people worked and slept and worried. A family's security could be seen in the morning light as clearly as the weather. It sat in the shed behind the house, in the field beyond the fence, in the tools laid out on a bench worn smooth by years of use. Ownership was physical, and because it was physical, it was understood.

Saving meant keeping things in motion. Animals had to be fed and bred. Land had to be tended season after season. Skills had to be practiced until they settled into muscle memory, the kind that stayed with you even when conditions turned harsh. A blacksmith, a carpenter, a farmer, a merchant did not think of wealth as a number that grew quietly in the background. Wealth was something that demanded attention. If it was neglected, it weakened. If it was respected, it endured.

Money existed, of course, but it occupied a modest role. Cash was a tool for exchange rather than a container for safety. It passed through hands on its way to something else. Grain. Iron. Labor. A roof repaired before winter. People understood, through experience rather than theory, that money by itself could vanish. A fire could take it. A thief could take it. A government could change its mind and take it. What lasted were the things money could be turned into before it lost its usefulness.

This is why independence mattered so deeply. It was practical. A household that could feed itself, fix what broke, and adapt when conditions shifted possessed a form of freedom that required no permission. Volatility was expected. Crops failed. Markets swung. The weather ruined careful plans. None of this was interpreted as injustice. It was the rhythm of life. Stability did not come from insulation against change. It came from the ability to respond to it.

Risk was woven into daily existence, yet it did not feel reckless. It felt familiar. People knew where they stood because the relationship between effort and outcome remained visible. Work created value in ways that could be observed without explanation. When you produced something useful, it improved your standing. When you failed to do so, the consequences arrived quickly and clearly. There was hardship in this arrangement, sometimes severe hardship, but there was also clarity. No one needed to decode the system to understand where they were within it.

Neighbors depended on one another in ways that were direct and reciprocal. Trust formed through repeated interaction rather than institutional assurance. If someone extended help, it was remembered. If someone broke faith, that too was remembered. Reputation functioned as currency. It could not be printed, outsourced, or repaired by distance.

In this world, the idea of separating labor from survival would have felt strange. Work was not a means to an abstract future. It was the ongoing act of maintaining a life. People did not expect guarantees. They expected responsibility. They did not ask whether the system was fair. They asked whether they could manage within it.

This did not make life easier. It made it intelligible.

What came later would promise relief from uncertainty, relief from exposure, relief from the constant demand to adapt. That promise would sound humane. It would sound progressive. It would sound like safety. Yet something subtle would be exchanged in the process. A form of sovereignty that had once lived in land, skill, and judgment would slowly migrate elsewhere. Decision-making would drift upward. Risk would be redistributed in ways that felt protective at first. Dependence would begin to wear the language of security.

Looking back, the shift can be difficult to see because it arrived dressed as improvement. The hardship of the old world is easier to remember than the autonomy it required. But autonomy was there, embedded in the ordinary mechanics of life. People understood the limits of their control, and within those limits, they exercised it fully.

What followed would offer something different. Fewer sharp edges. Fewer immediate consequences. More insulation between effort and outcome. For a time, this trade would feel like progress. Only much later would its cost become visible.

The safety that arrived did not appear from nowhere. It replaced something.

The Psychological Scar of the Depression

By the time the stock market collapsed in October of 1929, many families had already sensed that something was slipping. The newspapers had been full of confidence for years. America was modern now. Industrial. Efficient. Prosperous. Ordinary people had been invited into the market itself, encouraged to invest, to participate, to believe that progress was permanent. When prices began to fall, the initial reaction was disbelief rather than panic. Corrections were familiar. Crashes were supposed to be temporary.

What followed was not temporary.

Banks began to fail in waves, first in smaller towns, then in cities where confidence had once felt unshakable. By the early 1930s, thousands of banks had closed their doors, taking with them the savings of families who had done exactly what they were told. There was no insurance. No backstop. One day the money existed, and the next day it did not. The realization spread unevenly, carried by word of mouth and half-understood headlines, until it became impossible to ignore.

Breadlines appeared in neighborhoods where hunger had once felt distant. At first, people lined up quietly, coats pulled tight, faces forward, telling themselves this was a brief interruption. Fathers still left home early, still shaved, still wore the clothes that marked them as working men, even when there was nowhere left to report. The rituals mattered. They were a way of holding onto identity when income had already slipped away.

Unemployment rose with a speed that no one had prepared for. Factories slowed, then stopped. Farms produced food that could not be sold at prices high enough to justify harvest. Skilled laborers discovered that competence offered no protection when demand evaporated. By 1933, nearly a quarter of the workforce was without a job, and the number itself barely captured the damage. What collapsed was the belief that effort alone could keep a family safe.

Children absorbed the shift without understanding its mechanics. They noticed the smaller meals. The careful folding of worn clothes. The way parents spoke about money as if it were something dangerous, something that needed to be controlled lest it disappear again. They learned that security could vanish quickly and without explanation. That lesson lodged itself deeply, far deeper than any formal education.

When Franklin Roosevelt took office and declared a bank holiday in 1933, the gesture carried symbolic weight as much as economic intent. The government was stepping in, asserting control, promising order where chaos had reigned. New programs followed. Jobs were created. Deposits were eventually insured. Stability was rebuilt slowly, deliberately, and with an emphasis on preventing another collapse of confidence.

The fear had already done its work. People who had watched savings disappear did not easily trust abstractions again. They learned to value certainty over upside, predictability over possibility. The goal shifted toward avoiding loss rather than pursuing gain. These instincts were not debated or articulated. They were felt, reinforced each time scarcity threatened, each time memory resurfaced.

This generation did not pass down stories of risk. They passed down rules. Stay with what is stable. Keep what you earn. Do not rely on luck. Attach yourself to institutions that appear strong. These lessons were framed as wisdom because they had been learned under pressure. They carried the authority of survival.

When prosperity returned after the war, it did not erase these habits. It gave them a structure to live inside. Jobs that promised continuity felt like relief. Systems that absorbed uncertainty felt humane. Safety became something you entered rather than something you built. The fear receded into the background, no longer conscious, but still active.

This is how trauma becomes tradition. The original danger fades, but the behavior remains, reinforced by a world that temporarily rewards it. Children grow up internalizing caution without knowing its origin. They inherit a posture toward money and work shaped by events they never witnessed, guided by instincts that once made sense in a very different landscape.

Seen through this lens, the Depression was not just an economic collapse. It was a mass psychological event that rewired expectations around security, authority, and risk. It taught an entire generation what mattered most when everything else failed. Those lessons would go on to shape policy, culture, and family life for decades.

And they would eventually shape you.

When you recognize this inheritance, the choices your grandparents made begin to feel coherent rather than conservative. Their attachment to stability, their suspicion of risk, their loyalty to systems that promised order were not signs of small thinking. They were responses to a moment when the ground disappeared beneath them.

Understanding this does not require agreement. It requires recognition. The fear that organized their lives did not vanish when the economy recovered. It became embedded, carried forward quietly, shaping the world that followed, and the instincts you still carry today.

The Post-War Deal

When the war ended, the United States stood in an unusual position. Its industrial base was intact. Its competitors were rebuilding. Its population was exhausted but disciplined, accustomed to sacrifice, and ready for order. This was not a moment that invited experimentation. It invited design.

What followed was not accidental prosperity. It was a coordinated effort to prevent a return to the instability that had scarred the previous generation. Policymakers, institutions, and corporations shared a common goal, even if they expressed it in different language: restore confidence, reduce volatility, and keep the population anchored to predictable outcomes. Stability was no longer a byproduct of success. It became a target in its own right.

Jobs were structured to last. Large organizations expanded, offering long-term employment in exchange for loyalty. Pensions promised security at the end of a working life that followed a clear, linear path. Wages were steady. Inflation was managed. Credit was reshaped into something respectable, especially when attached to homes and education. Risk, once an accepted feature of economic life, was gradually framed as something that needed to be controlled, supervised, or avoided altogether.

Homeownership became central to this vision. A mortgage was not merely a loan. It was a mechanism of attachment. A homeowner was invested in continuity, in neighborhood stability, in rising values that depended on calm rather than disruption. Suburbs expanded, standardized and affordable, reinforcing a sense of progress that felt personal while remaining carefully contained.

Education followed a similar pattern. Standardized pathways promised mobility without encouraging deviation. The message was clear and reassuring: follow the sequence, meet the expectations, and your place would be waiting. Curiosity was welcome so long as it led to employability. Creativity was valued when it served existing structures. Independence was reframed as upward movement within the system rather than outside it.

None of this was presented as control. It was presented as care.

The memory of the Depression still lingered, even as prosperity spread. People wanted insulation from sudden loss. They wanted systems that absorbed shock on their behalf. In return, they accepted rules that limited unpredictability. Stability was not imposed by force. It was chosen willingly, reinforced by policies that rewarded compliance and by cultural signals that defined adulthood as responsibility, restraint, and reliability.

Risk slowly acquired a moral dimension. Taking chances came to be associated with immaturity, recklessness, or ingratitude. The ideal citizen did not disrupt. The ideal worker did not wander. The ideal adult built a life that could be forecast decades in advance. This predictability was framed as progress because it contrasted so sharply with the chaos that had come before.

The middle class emerged within this environment, not as a spontaneous outcome of hard work, but as a managed space between extremes. It functioned as a buffer, large enough to sustain consumption, production, and tax revenue, yet structured enough to remain dependent on wages rather than ownership. People did not need to control capital to feel secure. They needed access to systems that promised continuity.

This is where the concept becomes clearer. The middle class was not designed to maximize freedom. It was designed to minimize volatility. It reduced exposure to risk by spreading it across institutions. It traded autonomy for assurance. In doing so, it offered something many people wanted deeply: relief from uncertainty.

That relief came with conditions.

Work became something you did within predefined lanes. Wealth was accumulated indirectly through wages, pensions, and home equity rather than through direct ownership of productive assets. Decision-making shifted upward, away from households and toward organizations that set terms, benefits, and trajectories. People learned to optimize within the structure rather than question its shape.

This arrangement worked because the environment supported it. Global dominance allowed wages to rise alongside productivity. Debt remained manageable. Growth covered inefficiencies. The system delivered on its promises often enough to justify loyalty. For several decades, the bargain felt fair.

But the nature of the bargain matters more than its short-term success.

The middle class was not freedom. It was containment.

Not containment as punishment, but containment as design. It limited extremes. It softened shocks. It guided behavior toward outcomes that preserved order. It reduced the need for individuals to navigate uncertainty on their own by absorbing that uncertainty into institutions that appeared permanent.

Adulthood, within this framework, became synonymous with compliance. A responsible person followed the path. They trusted the system. They delayed gratification. They stayed within bounds. These traits were rewarded because they supported the larger goal of stability.

Few people stopped to ask what was being exchanged because the exchange felt reasonable. The pain of the past was still close enough to justify caution. The comfort of the present masked long-term costs. And the future appeared stable enough to make questioning seem unnecessary.

The deal succeeded precisely because it aligned fear with policy, memory with structure. It transformed a population shaped by collapse into one organized around predictability. It created a class that did not need to rebel because it had been promised protection.

What no one advertised was that this protection depended on conditions that could change. When those conditions shifted, the structure would remain, even as its guarantees quietly eroded.

That realization would come later.

The Lagging Behavior Trap

The world kept moving, even as the rules stayed in place.

At first, the changes were subtle enough to ignore. Wages still arrived on schedule. Careers still followed familiar paths. Saving still felt responsible. The language of adulthood remained intact, reinforced by parents, schools, employers, and financial advice that sounded reassuringly familiar. What had worked before was assumed to work again, simply because it always had.

Over time, however, the environment shifted in ways that were harder to explain but impossible to miss. Costs rose faster than incomes. Housing absorbed a larger share of earnings. Education required debt long before it produced security. Retirement plans changed shape, then quietly disappeared. Stability began to rely less on accumulated value and more on borrowed time.

The habits people relied on did not adjust at the same pace. Saving cash no longer preserved purchasing power. It slowly reduced it. Loyalty to employers no longer guaranteed continuity. Pensions gave way to individual responsibility framed as empowerment, even as risk increased. Debt, once approached cautiously, became the primary mechanism that kept households afloat.

None of this felt like a failure at first. It felt like personal inadequacy. People tightened budgets, delayed milestones, worked harder, blamed themselves for outcomes that seemed just out of reach. The assumption remained intact: if the system was not delivering, the problem must be individual.

This is where the trap closes.

Your grandparents learned how to survive a collapse. They learned to conserve, comply, and attach themselves to stability wherever it appeared. Those lessons were rational responses to the world they faced. You inherited those behaviors without inheriting the conditions that made them effective. The environment changed, but the instructions did not.

What once functioned as protection now quietly works against you. The discipline that preserved wealth now struggles to create it. The caution that once reduced risk now concentrates it. The obedience that once ensured inclusion now limits flexibility in a system that rewards mobility and leverage rather than patience.

This does not mean the old values were wrong. It means they were specific. They belonged to a particular moment, shaped by particular fears, embedded into a system that no longer operates the same way. Following them faithfully in a different landscape produces confusion rather than security.

The middle class is shrinking for reasons that have little to do with effort or character. People are working longer hours with higher credentials and greater stress, only to discover that the outcomes promised by the old deal arrive less often and with more conditions attached. The rules remain visible, but their effectiveness has faded.

Shame thrives in this gap. It convinces people that struggle is evidence of personal deficiency rather than structural drift. It keeps attention focused inward, away from the architecture that shapes outcomes. As long as individuals believe they are failing alone, the system remains unquestioned.

Understanding this changes the tone of the story. It replaces blame with clarity. The discomfort many people feel is not a sign that they missed something obvious. It is a signal that the instructions they were given no longer align with the environment they inhabit.

To see this clearly requires stepping further back than the Depression and further back than the post-war boom. It requires examining the moment when money began to separate from tangible value, when debt shifted from emergency tool to organizing principle, when inflation became subtle enough to ignore, and when labor gradually lost its ability to translate effort into ownership.

The middle class did not arise by accident. It was the result of deliberate choices made under pressure. And like any system, it reflects the priorities of its architects.

To understand why the rules stopped working, you have to understand how they were written.

That trail leads to a single year.
A single shift.
A quiet decision whose consequences unfolded slowly enough to feel inevitable.

1913.

The year everything changed.

CHAPTER 2

1913 - THE YEAR EVERYTHING CHANGED

Once Money Became Debt, Labor Became Collateral

In 1913, a man could work a full day and earn a dollar. Picture him for a moment. He wakes before sunrise. He walks to a factory, a rail yard, or a small workshop. He works with his hands. At the end of that day, he receives a silver coin or a paper note backed by gold. That dollar carries weight in his palm. It represents effort already spent. It can be exchanged for flour, meat, boots, lamp oil. It stores his labor in a compact form.

Now place that same dollar in your wallet today. It looks familiar. It still says "one dollar." The design changed. The ink changed. The paper changed. The number did not.

Yet according to long-term data from the U.S. Bureau of Labor Statistics, a dollar has lost roughly 96 to 97 percent of its purchasing power since 1913. A dollar today buys only a fraction of what it once did. This decline did not arrive through one dramatic event. It unfolded gradually across more than a century. The consequences compound quietly, year after year.

So what changed?

The worker still works. Effort still takes time. Skill still requires practice. The visible change is the money itself. To understand why that dollar changed, we have to step back into the world of 1913.

1913 did not feel revolutionary. There was no foreign invasion. There was no collapse of the banking system that year. No public sense that the economic foundation of the country was being rewritten. And yet, in that single year, Congress passed the Federal Reserve Act, signed into law on December 23, 1913. In the same year, the Sixteenth Amendment was ratified, authorizing a federal income tax.

Two legal changes. One concerning money creation. One concerning income. Taken together, they reshaped the structure of the American economy. To see why, we have to understand what money looked like before that moment.

In the late 19th and early 20th centuries, the United States operated under a version of the gold standard. Paper currency represented a claim on gold held in reserve. Banks issued notes and deposits, but those claims were constrained by the gold they held or could obtain. Gold did not expand quickly. Mining output increased slowly. That physical constraint limited how fast the money supply could grow.

Wealth during that period was closely tied to tangible production. Land produced crops. Factories produced goods. Railroads moved physical cargo. Ownership of productive assets determined income. Money functioned as a medium of exchange. It was a tool for transferring value that had already been created.

Banks did extend credit, and financial panics occurred during the 19th century. Yet the overall structure rested on a simple anchor: the supply of money was linked to a physical reserve. This structure carried advantages and constraints. It limited monetary expansion. It also created vulnerability during times of stress. When depositors demanded cash simultaneously, banks could struggle to meet withdrawals if reserves were insufficient.

That vulnerability became visible in 1907.

In October 1907, a failed attempt to corner the stock of United Copper Company triggered a wave of distrust in New York's financial markets. Depositors rushed to withdraw funds from banks and trust companies. Credit tightened. Liquidity evaporated. At that time, the United States had no central bank. No institution stood ready to inject reserves into the system during panic. Private financiers stepped in. J.P. Morgan gathered leading bankers in his library and coordinated emergency support for failing institutions. The crisis eventually stabilized, but the episode revealed structural fragility.

The lesson drawn by many policymakers was straightforward: the country needed a lender of last resort. It needed an "elastic currency," one that could expand during stress and contract during stability. In response, Congress established the National Monetary Commission. Lawmakers studied European central banks, particularly the Bank of England and the German Reichsbank. Reports were written. Debates followed. Over several years, proposals evolved into legislation.

By 1913, reform was ready.

The Federal Reserve Act created a central banking system composed of regional reserve banks overseen by a Board in Washington. Member banks would hold reserves at these regional banks. Federal Reserve Notes would become a standardized national currency. The system gained the authority to extend credit to banks during liquidity shortages. On paper, this was a technical reform designed to prevent future panics. In practice, it altered how money could be created.

Under the new system, money became more elastic. When banks issued loans, they created deposits in the borrower's account. These deposits functioned as money in the economy. The Federal Reserve could supply reserves to banks, influencing how much lending occurred by adjusting interest rates and reserve conditions.

To understand the importance of this shift, consider how bank lending works. When a bank approves a loan, it does not transfer physical gold bars from a vault into the borrower's hands. Instead, it credits the borrower's account with a deposit. That deposit becomes new purchasing power. On the bank's balance sheet, a loan appears as an asset. The borrower's promise to repay stands on the other side as a liability.

The principal amount of the loan enters circulation as money. The interest owed on that loan represents additional payment that must be earned over time. This structure means that money increasingly enters the economy through debt. Each new loan expands the money supply. Repayment extinguishes money. Expansion and contraction begin to follow the rhythm of credit creation.

Before this shift, money growth was constrained by gold production and reserves. After this shift, money growth became closely tied to lending activity. Money creation moved away from production and toward debt issuance. The system no longer required savings before lending. It required borrowers. This was a design choice made through legislation, shaped by the experience of financial panic.

The same year that centralized money creation was formalized, the Sixteenth Amendment authorized Congress to levy a federal income tax without apportioning it among the states. The federal government had previously relied heavily on tariffs and excise taxes for revenue. Income taxation created a direct and ongoing claim on wages and business profits.

This change also followed historical context. The Civil War had introduced a temporary income tax. That tax expired. Industrialization and expanding federal responsibilities increased pressure for a more stable revenue base. The amendment provided it.

Now place these two reforms side by side.

- One reform reshaped how money could be created.
- The other established a permanent mechanism for drawing revenue from labor and enterprise.

When money enters circulation through debt, repayment depends on income. When income becomes taxable at the federal level, a portion of that labor flows to support federal obligations, including interest payments on government debt. These connections unfold through accounting identities and policy decisions. They do not require hidden motives to function. They operate through structure.

Over the following decades, the United States experienced wars, depressions, and booms. The monetary system evolved further. Gold convertibility was adjusted in the 1930s. International gold exchange arrangements shifted after World War II. In 1971, the final link between the dollar and gold convertibility for foreign governments ended.

Across this century-long arc, the purchasing power of the dollar declined. Data from the Bureau of Labor Statistics show cumulative inflation eroding most of the dollar's value since 1913. This erosion occurred through many policy cycles. It reflected monetary expansion relative to goods and services. Inflation functions through arithmetic. When the supply of money grows faster than output, each unit represents a smaller share of total purchasing power. The effect often appears gradual in any single year. Over decades, it becomes visible.

The consequences compound quietly, year after year.

The deeper shift lies here. In a gold-constrained system, money primarily represented stored labor or stored production. In a credit-based system, money increasingly represents a claim on future labor. Loans finance homes, factories, vehicles, education. Repayment requires future income.

As credit expands, so does the aggregate claim on future earnings.

Once money became debt, labor became collateral.

This statement describes a structural relationship. If money enters circulation through lending, and if repayment depends on income, then the productive capacity of workers underwrites the system. The structure rewards expansion during growth periods. It also requires continued borrowing to sustain existing obligations.

In 1913, this design began in its modern form.

The grandfather's dollar did not change overnight. No headline announced that money would slowly detach from tangible anchors. The change occurred through law, institutional design, and policy tools that shaped incentives across generations.

If money is created through lending, then repayment must come from somewhere. That somewhere is the future effort of individuals and businesses. Understanding that shift prepares us for what follows.

From Ownership to Obligation

In the early years of the American republic, wealth was something you could point to. It stood in fields of wheat. It moved along rail lines. It hummed inside factories. Land produced food. Tools produced goods. Skills produced income. Money moved between these things as a medium of exchange. It helped coordinate activity. It did not sit at the center of the system as the product itself.

As the twentieth century unfolded, that relationship began to tilt. The change did not erase farms or factories. It shifted what determined the supply of money. After 1913, and especially in the decades that followed, money increasingly entered the economy through credit. A bank issued a loan. A deposit appeared in a borrower's account. Purchasing power expanded. The act of lending created money.

When the federal government runs a deficit, it issues Treasury securities. Investors purchase those securities. Banks and financial institutions hold them as assets. The Federal Reserve can purchase them in open market operations, increasing bank reserves. Through these channels, public debt integrates into the broader monetary system. In both cases, money enters as a liability somewhere on a balance sheet. The borrower promises repayment. The government commits to servicing its bonds. Income must eventually support those commitments.

As credit expands, so does the stock of money. As debt accumulates, so do claims on future labor.

This is where the shift from ownership to obligation becomes visible. Wealth still exists in tangible form. Yet the volume of money circulating through the economy increasingly reflects outstanding debt rather than stored metal or past production.

The system grows. It expands. It can function smoothly for long periods because borrowing finances homes, factories, roads, and education. Credit supports innovation and consumption. Growth makes repayment manageable. Expansion feels productive. The structure reveals its tension during a crisis.

By the early 1930s, the United States faced a severe contraction. Bank failures spread across the country. Depositors withdrew funds. Credit shrank. Output fell. Unemployment rose sharply. The monetary system, still linked to gold, came under strain.

In 1933, President Franklin D. Roosevelt signed Executive Order 6102, requiring Americans to surrender most forms of gold in exchange for paper currency. Shortly afterward, the government adjusted the official gold price, effectively devaluing the dollar relative to gold.

The stated purpose was stabilization. Gold convertibility constrained policy responses. By concentrating gold reserves and adjusting the dollar's gold price, the government gained greater flexibility to expand the money supply. The mechanism is straightforward. If each dollar must correspond to a fixed quantity of gold, monetary expansion remains limited by gold reserves. If convertibility rules change, the constraint loosens. Policy tools broaden.

During crisis, public tolerance for institutional change increases. Fear of economic collapse shifts priorities toward stability. Measures that alter monetary rules become acceptable when framed as necessary for recovery. After 1933, the United States remained connected to gold internationally, though domestic convertibility ended. The system evolved further after World War II through the Bretton Woods arrangement.

In 1944, representatives from allied nations met in Bretton Woods, New Hampshire, to design a postwar monetary framework. The agreement established the U.S. dollar as the central reserve currency, convertible into gold at $35 per ounce for foreign governments. Other currencies pegged to the dollar. This arrangement reflected economic realities. The United States held a large share of global gold reserves and industrial capacity after the war. Linking currencies to the dollar, and the dollar to gold, created a structured exchange system.

During the postwar decades, credit expanded domestically. Government spending supported infrastructure, housing, and defense. Private borrowing increased alongside rising incomes. The middle class grew. Industrial output expanded. Global trade deepened.

As long as gold reserves appeared sufficient to support international convertibility, the structure held. Over time, pressures accumulated. The United States ran balance-of-payments deficits. Dollars flowed abroad through military spending and foreign aid. Foreign central banks accumulated dollar reserves. Some began converting dollars into gold. The quantity of dollars held overseas grew relative to U.S. gold reserves.

The arithmetic tightened.

Where We Stand Now

If we step back from history and look at the present, the numbers tell a clear story.

As of this writing, U.S. federal debt exceeds $38 trillion. Credit card debt has surpassed $1 trillion. The United States operates with debt above 120 percent of GDP, meaning total federal obligations exceed the value of one full year of national economic output. These figures come from the U.S. Treasury and the Federal Reserve. They are published regularly. They are not abstract estimates. They are ledger entries.

Pause for a moment and bring this down to a personal scale.

If a household earned $100,000 per year and carried $120,000 or more in ongoing debt, year after year, lenders would examine its stability closely. If that household continued adding new debt to manage existing obligations, strain would build over time. Eventually income growth, spending cuts, or restructuring would become necessary.

Governments operate differently. A government that issues its own currency can finance obligations by issuing new debt that is ultimately supported by monetary expansion. Instead of defaulting outright, it can allow purchasing power to erode gradually. That erosion spreads across holders of currency and fixed-income assets.

That dilution is inflation. More on this in Chapter 4. But for now, just a basic understanding. Inflation is often described in headlines as rising prices. At its core, it reflects a decline in purchasing power tied to monetary expansion. When more dollars circulate relative to goods and services, each dollar commands a smaller share of output. This process does not require dramatic announcements. It unfolds through interest rate policy, deficit spending, asset purchases, and lending activity. You feel it in grocery bills, housing costs, tuition, insurance premiums. The numbers in your bank account may increase over time. The capacity of those numbers to buy stable amounts of goods changes.

A debt-based monetary system encourages borrowing to sustain growth. Government deficits add to the stock of outstanding obligations. Corporate leverage finances expansion and acquisitions. Households borrow for homes, education, and consumption. As long as credit expands, activity continues. When expansion slows, policymakers often respond with measures designed to encourage renewed borrowing.

A debt-based system can operate effectively for long stretches when growth offsets obligations. Over time, the scale of debt rises relative to output. Servicing that debt absorbs increasing shares of income and tax revenue. Policy choices narrow. When total obligations exceed annual economic output, as current debt-to-GDP ratios indicate, the system relies on continued borrowing, sustained growth, and manageable interest rates. Each of those variables interacts with the others.

As an individual, you cannot change national debt levels or central bank policy. You can understand the environment in which you operate. Once you see that money is created primarily through debt, several everyday observations begin to align.

You see why wages may struggle to outpace asset prices. Asset markets receive liquidity earlier in the transmission process. You see why holding large cash balances for long periods can erode purchasing power. Inflation reduces the real value of fixed sums over time. You see why access to low-cost credit often determines who can acquire appreciating assets.

A system built on expanding credit rewards those positioned near sources of new money. It pressures those dependent solely on wage income without asset ownership. It encourages participation in debt markets as a means of accessing opportunity. Over time, this shapes behavior. Households feel compelled to borrow for education to access higher-paying jobs. They borrow for housing because rents rise. They carry revolving credit when expenses exceed income. The sense of financial pressure often reflects structural incentives rather than personal failure.

You begin to see why wages lag, why prices rise, and why the middle class feels squeezed between obligations and aspirations. The system evolved through legislation, crisis response, and policy adaptation across a century. It functions according to design choices embedded in law and institutional practice.

We are living in one of the largest financial transitions in modern history. Wealth is shifting across sectors, asset classes, and generations. Some individuals position themselves close to expanding sources of credit. Others remain dependent on fixed incomes and depreciating purchasing power.

Once money became debt, labor became collateral. That sentence describes a relationship. When money enters the system as a liability, repayment depends on income. Your time and skill generate that income. Your paycheck represents purchasing power created within this broader structure.

You are paid in debt. Your paycheck feels like income in the traditional sense. Structurally, it represents a claim on a monetary system built through lending and policy decisions. It carries the imprint of balance sheets far beyond your employer.

When you grasp the nature of what you are being paid, you can ask better questions.

- How do assets behave in an expanding monetary environment?
- How does leverage alter outcomes?
- How does inflation affect long-term planning?

The quiet reforms of 1913 reshaped how money enters the economy. Over a century, that structure expanded, adapted, and compounded. Today's debt levels and monetary policies reflect that evolution.

The grandfather's dollar and your dollar share a name. Their purchasing power tells a longer story. To move forward, we need to examine what your paycheck actually represents inside this structure. That is where we go next.

CHAPTER 3

PAID IN DEBT

"You're paid in someone else's liability and charged interest for the privilege."

That sentence alone explains more about modern life than most economics textbooks.

The uncomfortable truth is this: most Americans do not realize what they are actually being paid. They believe their paycheck is income. In reality, it is a liability created somewhere else, issued as debt, and slowly eroded before it ever reaches them.

At 6:30 a.m., the alarm sounds. It is the same sound it has been for years. The rhythm of the morning is practiced. Shower. Coffee. Traffic. Badge scan. Desk. Screen. The structure feels familiar because it is familiar. Six to eight hours inside a building. Two short breaks and a lunch. Work that sometimes follows you home. Someone at the front of the room, only now the room is a department and the front is a corner office. There is still someone above them setting the rules.

When you were younger, your performance was marked in red ink. A letter at the top of a page. A number next to your name. You were graded, ranked, and evaluated. You stood in line. You raised your hand. You asked permission to speak. To leave. To use the restroom.

Today the symbols have changed, but the pattern remains. You receive performance reviews. You track quarterly targets. You watch metrics move on a dashboard. Eventually, someone checks your credit score. A different number. A different scale. The same feeling of being measured.

You ask permission for vacation. Permission to leave early. Permission to handle something personal. The structure did not disappear when you graduated. It expanded.

Around 9:14 a.m., your phone vibrates. A direct deposit notification. Payroll has cleared. The number looks solid. It looks earned. It feels like income. By Thursday, the number already feels smaller. Mortgage or rent has moved. Utilities have been drafted. Insurance has been deducted. Student loan autopay has been executed. Groceries cost a little more than last month. The paycheck feels like it passed through your account rather than settled in it.

Most people interpret this as a budgeting problem. A lifestyle problem.

There is another explanation.

To see it clearly, we have to zoom out for a moment into history.

In 1943, in the middle of World War II, Congress passed the Current Tax Payment Act. Before that year, most Americans paid their federal income taxes annually. You calculated what you owed and sent a payment. The 1943 law changed the timing and the mechanism. Employers began withholding federal income taxes directly from wages before workers received their pay. The government wanted steady revenue to finance wartime expenses. Withholding provided predictable cash flow.

This change reshaped the paycheck. Before withholding, a worker physically handled the full wage and later sent a portion to the government. After withholding, the worker received only the remainder. The paycheck became a pipeline. Income flowed through it, and institutions took their portion automatically.

The change was administrative. It was practical. It solved a wartime funding problem. It also had a psychological effect. When money is withheld before it reaches your hands, the transaction feels different. The deduction becomes routine. The system feels automatic. Over time, people stop thinking of their gross wage as something they ever truly possessed. The net amount becomes the reference point. The paycheck was no longer simply compensation from employer to worker. It became a distribution mechanism that moved money simultaneously toward households and toward the state.

That structural shift matters because it changed how Americans experienced income. It embedded obligation directly inside the act of earning. This pattern of embedding did not stop there.

Now here is the part most people never see. When you receive a direct deposit, it feels like your employer transferred existing money into your account. The intuitive picture is simple: the company earned revenue, stored it somewhere, and paid you from that stored pool.

Modern banking works differently. In today's monetary system, most money enters circulation through bank lending. When a commercial bank issues a loan - a mortgage, a business loan, an auto loan - it does not hand over pre-existing cash from a vault. It creates a deposit in the borrower's account. That deposit becomes new money in the economy. At the same time, the bank records a loan asset on its books. One side of the balance sheet shows the borrower's obligation. The other side shows the newly created deposit.

Central banks have described this process openly. The mechanics are accounting-based. Loans create deposits. This means that the total amount of money in circulation expands when borrowing expands. Deposits across the system increase as debt increases.

Your paycheck moves within that system.

When your employer pays you, the funds arrive as a bank deposit. That deposit is part of a broader pool of deposits that exists because loans have been issued somewhere in the system. Mortgages, business expansion loans, government bond purchases - these transactions collectively shape the quantity of deposits available.

Your income, in that sense, is a claim within a debt-linked structure. This does not mean your employer printed your paycheck. It means the monetary environment in which your employer operates - the availability of credit, the cost of borrowing, the volume of deposits in circulation - influences wages, prices, and cash flow.

In a debt-based monetary system, expansion in lending increases the supply of deposits. Over long periods, that expansion influences purchasing power. This is where the story becomes personal.

When you open your banking app and see a balance of $4,000, the number appears stable. It sits there quietly. It looks solid. Human beings are wired to anchor to visible numbers. Behavioral economists call this money illusion. We instinctively treat nominal values as if they reflect real value. A raise from $60,000 to $63,000 feels like clear progress because the number is larger.

The mind rarely adjusts automatically for changes in purchasing power. If the general price level rises over time - whether from increased money supply,

supply constraints, or demand pressures - the same number buys less. The number remains still. The purchasing power shifts.

This shift tends to occur gradually. Over decades, small annual changes compound. A modest inflation rate, repeated year after year, reduces what a fixed amount of currency can purchase. The effect does not announce itself dramatically. It accumulates.

When wages rise more slowly than living costs, workers feel pressure. The pressure feels personal because the paycheck is personal. It has your name on it. Yet the forces acting on that paycheck operate at the system level. Your labor is exchanged for a deposit. That deposit is part of a monetary structure in which new deposits are regularly created through lending. As the quantity of deposits grows over time, the share represented by each unit can shift.

Now return to the classroom. As a child, your value was measured by grades. You were evaluated on your ability to follow instructions, complete assignments, and perform within a defined structure. You were rewarded for compliance and consistency. The schedule trained you for a rhythm. Fixed hours. Authority at the front. Rules established above you.

As an adult, the evaluation tools changed. Instead of report cards, you receive performance reviews. Instead of GPA, you accumulate a credit score. Instead of detention, you face late fees or higher borrowing costs. Your financial identity becomes legible through a number tied to borrowing behavior.

This evolution did not occur by accident. As consumer credit expanded in the decades after World War II, lenders required scalable methods to evaluate millions of applicants. Standardized scoring models allowed that expansion. Borrowing became easier to distribute. Risk became easier to price. Debt became easier to normalize. Within this system, your ability to access housing, transportation, education, and sometimes employment connects to your history with credit.

The classroom prepared you to operate within structured evaluation. The workplace extended it. The credit system quantified it. Each layer reinforced the same rhythm: show up, perform, remain in good standing.

At this point, we have three pieces of history:

1. Payroll withholding embedded obligation inside income during the 1940s, reshaping how workers experience wages.

2. Modern banking structures create most deposits through lending, linking money supply expansion to debt issuance.
3. Standardized credit scoring scaled personal debt evaluation in the late twentieth century, turning borrowing behavior into a measurable identity.

Together, these developments form a pattern. Income flows through institutional channels automatically. Money enters the system primarily through debt expansion. Individuals are evaluated by how reliably they service debt. Within this framework, the paycheck feels like income earned and owned. Structurally, it functions as a claim inside a broader debt-linked system.

If money is created largely through lending, and if deposits expand when borrowing expands, and if individuals are evaluated based on their relationship to that borrowing, then the paycheck sits at the intersection of labor and leverage.

The question that follows is simple.

If you are paid in deposits that exist within an expanding debt structure, how does the system decide who benefits first from that expansion?

To answer that, we need to look at how evaluation shapes opportunity. That is where the report card returns - this time with interest attached.

The Adult Report Card

In 1989, a company called Fair, Isaac and Company introduced a standardized credit scoring model that could be used nationally. Lenders had long evaluated borrowers, but this model allowed them to do it quickly and consistently across millions of applications. A number between roughly 300 and 850 summarized a person's history with credit. That number estimated the probability that a borrower would repay a loan.

By the late twentieth century, consumer lending had expanded dramatically. Mortgages were widespread. Auto loans were common. Credit cards had become a normal part of household finance. Banks needed a way to price risk at scale. Manual underwriting worked in a smaller, slower system. Automated scoring worked in a fast, expanding one. The credit score solved a structural problem. If lending was going to grow, risk assessment had to become standardized.

From the lender's perspective, the logic is straightforward. Every loan carries the possibility of default. If lenders can measure the likelihood of repayment more precisely, they can price interest rates more precisely. Borrowers with stronger repayment histories receive lower rates. Borrowers with weaker histories receive higher rates. The number compresses complexity into something actionable.

From the borrower's perspective, the number becomes identity.

You begin to hear phrases like "I'm a 720" or "I need to get back above 700." The number travels with you when you apply for an apartment, a car, a mortgage. In some cases, employers review it as part of a background check. Insurance companies sometimes use credit-based scores in pricing policies.

A grade once determined access to advanced classes. A credit score determines access to capital. This shift fits within a larger financial expansion that unfolded over decades.

After World War II, the United States experienced strong economic growth, suburban expansion, and rising household formation. Government-backed mortgage programs made homeownership accessible to millions. Thirty-year fixed-rate mortgages became standard. Consumer credit began to support appliance purchases, automobiles, and later revolving credit through cards.

By the 1970s and 1980s, financial markets evolved further. Interest rate deregulation allowed banks to compete more aggressively. In 1980, the Depository Institutions Deregulation and Monetary Control Act phased out caps on interest rates that banks could pay depositors. Lending markets became more flexible. Credit cards spread rapidly.

During the 1980s and 1990s, securitization gained momentum. Banks increasingly bundled loans - especially mortgages - into securities that could be sold to investors. By moving loans off their balance sheets, banks freed up capacity to issue more loans. Risk was distributed across financial markets rather than concentrated in a single institution.

This process altered incentives. When loans could be packaged and sold, the originating lender's exposure to long-term default risk changed. Volume became important. Standardized scoring systems made volume manageable. More lending created more deposits. More deposits expanded the money supply. Expanded money supply supported asset purchases, including homes. Rising home values supported additional borrowing through refinancing and home equity loans. The cycle reinforced itself.

Household debt as a percentage of income increased over time. Mortgage balances grew. Student loan programs expanded. Auto financing terms lengthened. Debt became embedded in everyday life. Within that environment, the credit score served as a passport.

You are told to build credit. You open a card in college. You make small purchases. You pay on time. The score rises. You close an account and the score adjusts. You carry a balance and the utilization ratio shifts. A single late payment can move the number significantly.

The system communicates through feedback loops. If you repay consistently, borrowing becomes cheaper. Cheaper borrowing allows larger purchases. Larger purchases may require additional borrowing. Each step deepens participation.

This structure changes how worth is interpreted. When you were graded in school, the measurement focused on academic output. In the adult financial system, measurement focuses on repayment behavior. Production still matters. Income determines how much debt you can service. Yet the score does not directly measure what you produce. It measures how reliably you service obligations.

Credit score does not equal wealth. It equals borrowability. A person with substantial assets and minimal debt may have a modest score if they rarely use credit. A person with moderate income and steady repayment history may have a high score despite limited net worth.

The number signals compatibility with the lending system. This matters because modern economies rely heavily on credit expansion. When banks issue loans, deposits are created. Those deposits circulate. They fund payrolls, purchases, and investment. As long as loans are serviced, the system remains stable. When defaults rise sharply, stress spreads.

The financial crisis of 2008 illustrates this mechanism clearly.

In the early 2000s, mortgage lending expanded rapidly. Low interest rates, financial innovation, and securitization encouraged homeownership and speculative investment. Lenders extended credit to a wider range of borrowers, including those with weaker repayment histories. Adjustable-rate mortgages and complex loan structures became common.

Home prices rose steadily for several years. Rising prices allowed refinancing. Refinancing allowed additional borrowing. The cycle appeared sustainable as long as prices increased.

When housing prices slowed and then declined, many borrowers found themselves with mortgages larger than the value of their homes. Adjustable rates reset higher. Delinquencies increased. Securities backed by those mortgages lost value. Financial institutions that held or guaranteed them faced large losses.

Credit markets tightened. Lending slowed. Because lending creates deposits, a slowdown in credit growth affects the broader economy. Construction declined. Unemployment rose. Households reduced spending.

The crisis revealed how deeply household balance sheets were intertwined with financial markets.

After 2008, regulators strengthened capital requirements for banks. The Dodd-Frank Act introduced new oversight mechanisms. Yet the underlying structure remained: credit plays a central role in money creation and economic expansion. For individuals, the lesson was immediate. A strong credit score preserved access to refinancing options and lower rates. A damaged score limited choices. The adult report card determined flexibility.

There is a psychological dimension to this environment.

Research in behavioral economics and psychology shows that financial scarcity consumes mental bandwidth. When bills accumulate and due dates approach, attention narrows. Cognitive resources shift toward urgent problems. Long-term planning becomes harder. Decision fatigue increases.

In one well-known study, researchers found that when individuals were prompted to think about large, unexpected expenses, their performance on cognitive tasks temporarily declined. The effect was similar to losing several hours of sleep. The mechanism appears linked to stress and preoccupation.

Debt amplifies this dynamic. A household carrying high-interest balances must allocate attention to payment schedules, interest accrual, and potential penalties. The focus becomes immediate survival within the billing cycle.

This pattern helps explain why financial strain often leads to reactive decisions. Taking on a short-term loan to cover a shortfall may resolve today's stress while increasing future obligations. The decision can appear rational within a narrow time frame.

When observers interpret these choices as irresponsibility, they overlook structural context. A system that normalizes borrowing, prices risk continuously, and rewards steady repayment places individuals in a constant evaluation loop.

You were trained to perform within evaluation systems. Now the evaluation involves interest rates. The list of adult expectations reinforces this rhythm:

- Get a job.
- Get benefits.
- Enroll in a 401(k).
- Maintain insurance.
- Stay loyal.
- Stick it out.

Each item ties you more closely to institutional channels. A job provides income. Income supports debt service. Debt service sustains credit score. Credit score preserves access to future borrowing. Retirement accounts tie long-term security to market performance. Insurance manages risk exposure.

When borrowing expands across society, deposits expand. As deposits expand over long periods, purchasing power can shift. If wages do not keep pace with the cost of housing, education, healthcare, and other essentials, households rely more heavily on credit to bridge gaps. Borrowing becomes a tool for smoothing consumption.

This creates a feedback loop.

- Borrowing increases money supply.
- Expanded money supply supports asset demand.
- Asset prices rise.
- Rising asset prices require larger loans for new buyers.
- Larger loans increase debt balances.
- Servicing those balances requires steady income.
- Steady income requires continued participation in the labor market.

The system depends on reliable participants. Your worth, in this context, is measured partly by how predictably you can service obligations. The credit score quantifies that predictability. It converts your payment history into a signal that lenders and institutions can use.

Over time, participation becomes normalized. A young adult enters the workforce with student loans. They rent an apartment that requires a credit check. They finance a car to commute. They open a credit card to build history. Each step deepens integration into the lending system.

The system continues functioning as long as participants continue servicing obligations.

You were not trained to question the structure. You were trained to succeed within it. The adult report card makes that success measurable. The next question follows naturally.

If your identity is shaped by how well you carry debt, and if money itself expands through debt, what happens to the purchasing power of the deposits you earn?

To answer that, we need to examine how expansion influences value over time.

A Claim Inside a System

Let's talk about wages in practical terms.

If your salary increases from $50,000 to $55,000 over several years, you experience progress. The number rises. The deposit is larger. On paper, income has grown. Economists distinguish between nominal wages and real wages. Nominal wages are the dollar amount printed on your pay stub. Real wages adjust that number for changes in the overall price level.

Data from the Bureau of Labor Statistics tracks average hourly earnings over time. When those earnings are adjusted for inflation, the growth pattern looks different from the nominal line. Some periods show meaningful gains. Other periods show slow growth. In certain stretches, real purchasing power remains flat even while nominal wages rise.

You do not need a chart to feel this. You feel it when rent increases faster than your paycheck. You feel it when insurance premiums rise while your salary review adds a modest percentage. You feel it when the cost of education, childcare, or healthcare takes a larger share of income than it did a decade ago.

The arithmetic is simple. If prices grow at 3 percent per year and wages grow at 2 percent per year, purchasing power narrows over time. The difference compounds quietly. When money supply expands through lending and deficit spending, more deposits circulate. Those deposits compete for goods, services, and assets. Prices respond over time to supply and demand conditions, including the availability of credit.

If asset prices - homes, equities, investment properties - rise faster than wages, access becomes more difficult for those who rely primarily on labor income.

This is where middle-class pressure begins to show.

The modern financial system rewards participation in predictable ways. If you earn wages, deposit them in a bank, and service your obligations on time, you maintain access to credit. Access to credit allows you to purchase a home, finance a car, smooth income shocks, and invest through retirement accounts. This pathway works best when income growth keeps pace with asset growth and when borrowing costs remain manageable.

Over the past several decades, asset prices have often grown faster than median wages. Housing in major metropolitan areas provides one example. Stock market indices have compounded over long periods, reflecting corporate earnings growth and reinvestment. Households that owned these assets early participated directly in that growth.

Households that entered later faced higher entry prices and larger required loans. When assets appreciate, the owners benefit. When borrowing is inexpensive, leveraged asset ownership can amplify gains. A homeowner who purchases a property with a 20 percent down payment controls the full value of the asset while financing the remainder. If the home value rises, the equity grows faster than the original cash invested.

This mechanism explains how leverage can accelerate wealth accumulation for asset holders.

It also explains why entry timing matters. If you rely primarily on wages and keep savings in cash deposits, your financial position grows at the pace of income. If asset prices grow faster than income, the gap widens over time. This dynamic contributes to wealth concentration.

Wealth data from the Federal Reserve's Survey of Consumer Finances shows that households in higher wealth percentiles hold a larger share of financial assets, including equities and business ownership. These assets historically appreciate over long horizons. Middle-income households hold a larger share of their wealth in primary residences and cash-like assets. Lower-income households hold limited financial assets and rely heavily on labor income.

When monetary expansion supports asset markets - whether through lower interest rates, quantitative easing, or sustained credit growth - asset holders experience gains earlier in the cycle. Wage adjustments typically occur more slowly.

Now consider the psychological dimension.

Financial anxiety correlates with measurable stress. Surveys conducted by organizations such as the American Psychological Association consistently report money as a leading source of stress for adults. Debt levels, uncertainty about retirement, and rising costs contribute to this pressure. When obligations extend years into the future - mortgage terms of thirty years, student loan repayment schedules spanning decades - they shape present behavior. Career decisions become linked to benefit packages and income stability. Risk tolerance narrows when fixed expenses are high.

If your monthly obligations consume a large portion of income, preserving steady cash flow becomes central. You remain in roles that provide reliability. You prioritize predictability. You postpone experiments that might disrupt income. The system rewards that stability because steady income supports steady debt service. Steady debt service supports bank balance sheets. Stable banks support financial markets. Stable markets support economic confidence.

Your individual behavior fits into that larger feedback loop.

Over time, this alignment can feel constraining. You save in currency that yields modest returns. Asset prices rise at a faster pace. You increase contributions to retirement accounts invested in markets, accepting volatility in exchange for growth potential. You manage credit carefully to preserve optionality.

You are navigating within a system designed around expansion and repayment. Understanding this structure shifts the conversation from blame to positioning.

When you position yourself closer to appreciating assets and manage liabilities strategically, you change your relationship to expansion. You participate in growth rather than absorbing its side effects.

This is practical, not ideological.

It means asking questions such as:

- How much of my income is tied exclusively to labor?
- How much of my balance sheet consists of assets that can grow?
- What interest rates am I paying relative to expected returns?
- How exposed am I to rising costs without offsetting income?

These questions move you from participant to informed participant.

Now, imagine that same morning again. The alarm sounds. You prepare for work. The deposit arrives. Nothing about that scene changes overnight. What changes is interpretation. You recognize that the deposit represents a claim within a debt-linked monetary structure. You understand that its purchasing power depends on broader economic conditions. You see that your credit score functions as a gateway to borrowing. You understand that asset ownership alters your exposure to expansion.

You stop interpreting every financial pressure as a personal failing. You start viewing it as a structural position. This perspective brings steadiness. You were trained to operate inside structured systems. You learned to follow schedules, meet benchmarks, and maintain standing. Those skills remain useful. They become more powerful when paired with structural awareness.

Being paid in debt explains part of the tension many people feel. The other part involves how that debt is created, how quickly it expands, and who receives it first.

That deeper layer requires understanding the mechanism itself.

- How money enters the system.
- How central banks influence liquidity.
- How expansion translates into asset prices.
- How inflation moves through different sectors at different speeds.

That exploration comes next. For now, hold this clear idea: Your paycheck is real. Your effort is real. The pressures you feel have structural roots. When you see the structure, you gain options. Being paid in debt is only part of the equation.

CHAPTER 4

INFLATION - THE SILENT TAX

On a quiet Tuesday night, Daniel sits at his kitchen table with his phone in his hand. He opens his banking app and looks at the number on the screen: **$10,000**. It feels solid. Round numbers often do. Ten thousand sounds like progress. It feels like something built carefully, month by month. Daniel thinks about the overtime shifts he picked up last year. He thinks about the weekend he stayed home instead of traveling. The number represents effort. It represents discipline.

A week later, he goes to the grocery store. The total at checkout is higher than he remembers. He notices it but shrugs. Prices rise. That happens. A month later, his landlord sends a renewal notice. Rent is going up again. The insurance premium for his car adjusts upward. A routine doctor visit costs more than the previous year. The school program his niece attends raises its annual fee. Each increase arrives quietly. No announcement. No vote. No separate invoice labeled "inflation." The $10,000 still reads $10,000. The number does not blink or flicker. It sits there calmly.

Yet what that number can buy has shifted. This is the nature of inflation. It does not show up as a bill in the mail. It does not require a ballot. It does not appear as a deduction on a paycheck. It shows up in prices. It shows up in grocery aisles, rent renewals, insurance statements, tuition invoices, and medical bills.

The phrase often repeated is simple: "Inflation doesn't hit everyone equally. It punishes savers and rewards insiders." The line can sound dramatic, but it describes a structural pattern that has repeated across monetary history. When money expands, the effect moves through the economy in a sequence. That sequence shapes outcomes.

Daniel is not thinking about monetary history. He is thinking about his budget. He looks again at the $10,000 and feels the comfort of seeing the same number.

Human beings anchor to visible figures. A number on a screen feels fixed. It feels stable. Yet money represents purchasing power, not ink or pixels. When the total supply of money in an economy expands faster than the production of goods and services, each unit of currency represents a slightly smaller claim on real output. The number can remain unchanged while its economic meaning evolves.

Central banks in advanced economies have often described a modest level of inflation, around 2 to 3 percent per year, as consistent with economic stability. A steady 3 percent annual increase in prices might appear small in isolation. Over time, however, compounding changes the picture. At 3 percent inflation, purchasing power declines by roughly half in about 24 years. This is arithmetic, not opinion. A dollar today buys half as much in roughly a quarter century if that rate persists.

Consider Daniel's $10,000 under that framework. If inflation averages 3 percent per year and the funds sit untouched for 24 years, the purchasing power of that sum would be equivalent to about $5,000 in today's terms. The screen would still show five digits. The economic weight behind those digits would have shifted.

Now add wages to the picture. Suppose Daniel's salary increases by 2 percent annually while inflation runs at 3 percent. His paycheck grows in nominal terms. The number printed on his pay stub increases. Yet his real purchasing power declines by roughly 1 percent each year. After a decade, that gap compounds. He works harder. He earns more in nominal dollars. His ability to buy goods and services edges backward. This arithmetic explains why many people feel stuck despite consistent effort. The experience is not imaginary. It reflects the difference between nominal income and real income.

The tendency to focus on the number rather than its purchasing power has a long intellectual history. In the early twentieth century, economist Irving Fisher described what he called "money illusion." People evaluate their financial well-being based on the face value of money rather than its real value adjusted for prices. If a worker receives a 2 percent raise during a year when inflation runs at 3 percent, the raise feels positive. The paycheck is larger. The illusion arises because the reference point is the visible number rather than the basket of goods that number can purchase.

This psychological pattern makes inflation difficult to see in its early stages. The balance in a bank account appears steady. Salaries often rise gradually. Prices increase at different speeds across categories. Groceries may climb faster than electronics. Rent may rise faster than clothing. The changes are dispersed across daily life. There is rarely a single moment when inflation announces itself clearly. Instead, it accumulates through many small adjustments.

To test this in your own life, consider a simple comparison. Think about what your regular grocery basket cost two years ago. Think about your rent or mortgage payment at your last renewal. Think about health insurance premiums or tuition invoices. The changes may not have occurred all at once. They may have moved in steps. Each step can be traced to a mixture of supply conditions, demand pressures, wage trends, and monetary expansion.

Inflation does not require dramatic headlines to operate. A steady 3 percent rate changes the economic landscape over a generation. A 1 percent gap between wage growth and inflation alters living standards slowly. These shifts accumulate quietly. This section lays the foundation for a larger question. If inflation changes purchasing power over time, and if money can expand through policy and credit, then its impact may depend on where someone sits within that system. Daniel experiences inflation through prices. Others encounter it at earlier stages, when new money enters the financial system.

Understanding that sequence requires looking at who receives new money first, how it moves through markets, and why timing matters. If inflation reshapes purchasing power, the order in which it travels shapes opportunity.

That is where we turn next.

Who Feels It First, Who Feels It Last

If new money enters the system, where does it go first?

That question sounds simple. It turns out to be the key to understanding why inflation feels uneven. When most people think about inflation, they imagine prices rising across the board at the same time. Groceries cost more. Rent costs more. Insurance costs more. It feels broad and universal. The lived experience creates the impression that inflation spreads evenly, like water filling a container.

The financial system works differently. Money enters specific places first. It moves through identifiable channels. It reaches some balance sheets before others. That order shapes outcomes long before grocery prices change.

To see this clearly, we have to follow the mechanics step by step.

In modern economies, most new money is created through credit. When commercial banks extend loans, they create deposits. When central banks purchase financial assets or lower interest rates, they increase reserves and encourage lending. When governments run deficits and issue bonds, they draw funds into the financial system that may be supported by central bank operations. Each of these actions expands the supply of money or credit in some form.

The first recipients of newly created money are typically financial institutions, large borrowers, and governments. Banks receive reserves. Institutional investors receive proceeds from asset sales. Corporations issue bonds at lower rates. Governments finance spending through debt markets.

At this early stage, prices in everyday consumer markets have not yet adjusted. The new money is still concentrated in financial channels. It flows into securities, bonds, real estate transactions, and large capital projects. Asset markets tend to respond first because they are directly connected to credit conditions.

This sequence has been observed for centuries. In the eighteenth century, the economist Richard Cantillon described how new money entering an economy affects different groups at different times. Those who receive it first can spend at existing prices. As the money circulates, prices begin to adjust. Later recipients encounter higher prices before their own incomes rise. This pattern has come to be known as the Cantillon Effect.

The principle does not rely on ideology. It describes timing. Consider a simplified example. Suppose the central bank lowers interest rates sharply. Borrowing becomes cheaper. Large firms refinance debt at lower costs. Private equity funds access credit at favorable rates. Investors purchase assets using leverage. Demand for financial assets rises. Stock prices increase. Real estate values climb. Bond yields fall.

At this stage, grocery prices have not necessarily moved. Wage contracts have not automatically adjusted. The new credit has entered the financial layer first. Over time, as asset values rise, several things follow. Homeowners see property values increase. Corporations with higher stock prices find it easier to raise capital. Investors experience gains that can be reinvested. Some of that wealth eventually translates into spending. When spending broadens and money supply growth exceeds real output growth, consumer prices begin to respond more visibly.

The order matters because early recipients can deploy funds before price adjustments ripple outward. This sequence was visible after the financial crisis of 2007–2008. When credit markets froze and major institutions faced insolvency, central banks stepped in with large-scale interventions. In the United States, the Federal Reserve lowered its policy rate close to zero and began purchasing large quantities of Treasury securities and mortgage-backed securities in what became known as quantitative easing.

The stated goal was to stabilize financial markets, lower long-term interest rates, and support economic recovery. The Federal Reserve's balance sheet expanded significantly during this period. Bank reserves increased. Liquidity in financial markets improved. Asset prices responded.

From 2009 onward, major equity indices recovered and then rose substantially over the following decade. Housing markets, after an initial collapse, also regained strength in many regions as mortgage rates fell and credit conditions stabilized. Asset values increased more rapidly than median wages.

Wage growth did occur during the recovery. It proceeded gradually. Consumer price inflation during much of the 2010s remained relatively subdued by historical standards, often near or slightly below the Federal Reserve's 2 percent target. Yet asset inflation moved on a different trajectory. Stocks and real estate experienced substantial appreciation over the same period.

The divergence illustrates the sequence described earlier. Liquidity entered financial markets directly. Asset holders experienced price increases early. Wage earners experienced improvements later and at a slower pace.

Now consider what this means for someone holding cash.

In a monetary system where money supply expands over time, cash sitting idle tends to lose purchasing power if inflation persists. The erosion may be gradual, especially during periods of moderate inflation. Over long stretches, the effect compounds.

Previous generations often emphasized saving money in bank accounts as a cornerstone of financial stability. In eras of lower inflation and higher real interest rates on deposits, savings accounts could preserve or modestly increase purchasing power. In periods when nominal interest rates fall below inflation, depositors experience negative real returns. The account balance may grow slightly in nominal terms. The purchasing power can still decline. This dynamic helps explain why some people feel disciplined yet fall behind. They follow traditional advice. They save. They avoid excessive consumption. They see modest nominal gains in their accounts. Over time, the real value shifts in the opposite direction.

Asset owners operate under different arithmetic. If an asset appreciates at a rate exceeding inflation, it preserves or increases real purchasing power. If leverage is used carefully, returns can amplify. Borrowing at low interest rates to acquire assets that rise faster than the cost of debt can create compounding effects. The same credit expansion that erodes cash balances can support asset appreciation. This is where leverage enters the picture.

Leverage magnifies outcomes. When borrowing costs decline due to monetary policy, institutions with access to low-cost credit can acquire assets more easily. A real estate investment trust can finance property purchases at favorable rates. A corporation can issue bonds to repurchase shares. A private equity fund can structure acquisitions using borrowed funds. When asset prices rise, leveraged positions benefit disproportionately relative to unleveraged cash holdings. The system channels gains toward those positioned closest to credit expansion.

The measurement of inflation also shapes perception. Most countries track consumer price inflation using indices designed to reflect a representative basket of goods and services. In the United States, the Consumer Price Index measures changes in prices for items such as food, housing, transportation, medical care, and other household expenses. The index serves important functions. It informs monetary policy decisions and cost-of-living adjustments.

At the same time, asset prices such as stocks and real estate are not directly included in consumer price indices. Housing costs are represented through components such as rent and owners' equivalent rent rather than through actual home sale prices. As a result, rapid increases in asset values can occur alongside relatively modest consumer price inflation readings.

For households, housing often represents the largest expense or asset. When home prices rise faster than rents or wages, affordability changes even if headline inflation appears moderate. Education and healthcare costs can also increase at rates exceeding the general inflation index. Insurance premiums may rise due to underwriting adjustments and risk pricing independent of general CPI trends.

This divergence between measured inflation and lived cost pressures contributes to confusion. When official statistics report inflation at 2 or 3 percent, individuals may still experience higher effective increases in their largest expense categories. The gap between measurement and experience fosters a sense of dislocation.

Two psychological tendencies reinforce this dynamic.

The first is fairness bias. People tend to assume that economic changes affect everyone similarly. If inflation is reported at 3 percent, the intuitive expectation is that prices rise evenly by roughly that amount across categories and groups. In practice, price movements vary by sector, region, and timing. Asset holders, renters, homeowners, and wage earners experience inflation differently.

The second is visibility bias. Consumers notice price changes in frequently purchased items such as food and gasoline. They pay less attention to asset inflation until it affects entry barriers. A young family may realize the impact of housing inflation when attempting to buy their first home. By that point, asset prices have already adjusted significantly.

You may have noticed this sequence in recent years. Headlines may report that inflation is cooling from a previous peak. Grocery bills may stabilize at a higher plateau rather than return to earlier levels. Rent renewals may lock in elevated rates. Stock markets may recover swiftly after downturns, while wage negotiations proceed slowly. Each of these patterns reflects timing. Inflation moves through layers. Financial markets respond quickly to credit conditions. Labor markets adjust more gradually due to contracts, bargaining processes, and productivity trends. Consumer prices often respond with a lag as businesses pass through input costs.

The result is a layered experience. Those positioned near credit expansion can act early. Those dependent primarily on wages encounter adjustments later. This layered structure creates tension within the system, though the tension arises from mechanics rather than intent. As debt expands to support growth, asset markets absorb liquidity. As liquidity circulates, prices adjust. Over time, the distribution of gains reflects the sequence of entry points.

If this pattern has unfolded repeatedly in modern monetary history, a natural question follows.

Has it always operated at the same speed?

To answer that, we need to examine a moment when the constraints on money changed more fundamentally and the pace of expansion shifted. That turning point lies in the early 1970s.

1971 and the World That Followed

If you want to understand why the pace of inflation changed, you have to stand in August of 1971.

Up to that point, the United States operated under the Bretton Woods system. The dollar was linked to gold at a fixed rate of $35 per ounce, and other major currencies were linked to the dollar. Foreign governments could exchange dollars for gold through official channels. This arrangement did not eliminate inflation. It did create an external reference point. Gold convertibility acted as a boundary condition. It required policymakers to consider gold reserves when expanding the money supply.

In August 1971, President Richard Nixon announced that the United States would suspend the dollar's convertibility into gold. The decision was described as temporary. It became permanent. From that moment forward, the dollar was backed by confidence and policy rather than a fixed claim on a metal reserve.

That shift removed a primary constraint on money creation. When currency is not convertible into a physical asset, expansion depends on credit conditions, fiscal policy, and central bank decisions. The flexibility offers advantages. It allows governments and central banks to respond to recessions, financial crises, and wars with greater speed. It also changes the long-term dynamics of debt and inflation.

Once convertibility ended, debt expansion became structurally easier. Governments could run deficits without the same pressure on gold reserves. Central banks could adjust interest rates and expand balance sheets without worrying about maintaining a fixed gold parity. Commercial banks continued to create deposits through lending. The system became more elastic.

Elastic systems tend to grow.

During the decades that followed, federal debt expanded significantly. Deficits became part of normal fiscal policy rather than rare emergency measures. Periods of economic stress, such as recessions and financial crises, were met with monetary easing and additional borrowing. Over time, this pattern reinforced itself. Growth supported borrowing. Borrowing supported spending. Spending supported growth.

Asset prices moved within this environment. When interest rates decline, the present value of future cash flows rises. Stocks become more valuable because future earnings are discounted at lower rates. Real estate becomes more affordable on a monthly payment basis when mortgage rates fall. Bond prices increase as yields decline. Each round of monetary easing tends to lift asset valuations through this mechanical relationship.

Over decades, this compounding effect becomes visible in charts of stock indices and housing prices. Asset appreciation outpaced wage growth for extended stretches, especially from the early 1980s onward. That divergence matters because ownership of financial assets is unevenly distributed across households. Families who own appreciating assets participate in that compounding. Families whose primary income comes from wages experience a different trajectory.

The 1970s offered a vivid lesson in how inflation can accelerate when money and credit expand rapidly. After the end of gold convertibility, the United States experienced a combination of fiscal deficits, oil price shocks, and accommodative monetary policy. Consumer price inflation rose sharply. By the late 1970s, annual inflation reached double digits.

High inflation changes behavior quickly. Contracts shorten. Lenders demand higher interest rates to compensate for expected price increases. Workers push for higher wages to preserve purchasing power. Businesses adjust prices more frequently. The pace of economic life accelerates.

In 1979, Paul Volcker became Chairman of the Federal Reserve. He raised interest rates aggressively, with the federal funds rate peaking above 19 percent in the early 1980s. The policy induced a severe recession. It also brought inflation down over time. The episode demonstrated that inflation, once embedded, requires forceful tightening to reverse. It also showed the social cost of such tightening. Unemployment rose sharply. Businesses failed. Borrowers faced high financing costs.

The lesson from that period is structural. Inflation can accelerate in a flexible monetary system. Reducing it can require painful adjustments. Policymakers therefore face trade-offs. The flexibility introduced after 1971 allows stabilization during crises. It also permits sustained debt growth and periodic inflationary pressure.

Fast forward to the present.

The United States now operates with federal debt exceeding $38 trillion. Consumer credit card debt stands above $1 trillion. The national debt-to-GDP ratio exceeds 120 percent. These figures are reported by the U.S. Treasury and other official sources. They describe scale. They also describe structure.

When debt grows faster than national income for extended periods, the system relies on continued expansion, higher nominal growth, higher inflation, or some form of restructuring to manage the burden. Governments can roll over debt by issuing new bonds. Central banks can influence interest rates to manage servicing costs. Inflation can reduce the real value of outstanding obligations over time.

From a structural standpoint, inflation becomes one of the adjustment mechanisms available within a high-debt system. Moderate inflation reduces the real burden of fixed-rate debt. It erodes the purchasing power of cash savings. It alters the relationship between wages, prices, and asset values.

This dynamic places pressure on the middle of the income distribution. Households that rely primarily on wages and hold a large share of their savings in cash or low-yield accounts experience the erosion first. Households that own appreciating assets and have access to credit participate in the expansion more directly. The effect accumulates slowly. A family may respond to rising costs by working additional hours. They may delay large purchases. They may refinance debt when rates are favorable. They adjust to the environment. The adjustments feel personal. The underlying forces are structural.

When money loses value gradually, people adapt their expectations. They accept that housing costs rise faster than income. They assume that education will require larger loans. They expect healthcare expenses to increase each year. These expectations shape life decisions. Career choices, family planning, geographic mobility, and risk tolerance are all influenced by perceived financial stability.

Over time, the middle class feels pressure from both sides. Asset prices rise, making entry more difficult for first-time buyers. Wages grow, though often at a pace that struggles to match key expenses. Debt becomes a bridge between current income and desired consumption. Mortgages stretch longer. Student loans extend decades. Credit cards fill temporary gaps.

The concentration of wealth intensifies through compounding. When asset values appreciate over decades and ownership is concentrated, the gains accrue unevenly. The mechanism does not require intent. It follows from mathematics. A portfolio that compounds at rates exceeding inflation grows faster than a wage that lags price increases. Access to leverage amplifies the effect.

You may have sensed this pattern without naming it. You may have noticed that markets recover swiftly after downturns while household budgets recover more slowly. You may have observed that housing affordability changes faster than salary bands. You may have experienced the feeling that progress requires more effort than it once did.

These experiences connect to the structural shift that began in 1971 and accelerated through subsequent decades of credit expansion.

This brings us to what might be called the real divide.

Public conversations often frame economic tension as left versus right or rich versus poor. Those categories capture political and social debates. The structural divide in a monetary system that expands through credit looks different. It centers on financial literacy versus financial dependence.

Financial literacy, in this context, means understanding how monetary cycles influence asset prices, wages, and debt. It means recognizing that cash loses purchasing power in an expanding system. It means understanding how interest rates affect valuations and borrowing costs. It involves positioning income and savings in ways that account for inflation rather than ignoring it. Financial dependence, by contrast, describes reliance on wages alone while holding most savings in forms that do not outpace inflation. It describes participation at the end of the money chain, where price adjustments arrive before income adjustments.

The middle class feels pressure when it occupies the space between rising asset values and slower wage growth. Families strive to save, to invest, to secure homes, and to educate children within a system where prices adjust continuously. The finish line appears to move because the unit of measurement itself changes over time.

Recognizing this structure changes how you interpret your own experience. When expenses rise faster than wages, the gap reflects broader forces at work. When asset prices climb during periods of monetary easing, the mechanism follows from discounted cash flow mathematics and credit availability. When debt levels expand nationally, inflation becomes one of the adjustment variables available to policymakers.

This chapter is meant to orient you within that landscape. Inflation reduces purchasing power over time. Debt expansion and flexible monetary policy enable that process. Asset ownership interacts with credit conditions to shape wealth distribution. These relationships follow from arithmetic and policy structure rather than personal failure.

To understand why insiders often move first, you must see how money is born, how it flows, and who stands closest to the source.

CHAPTER 5

HOW MONEY IS CREATED?

On a Tuesday afternoon in early spring, Jacob and Marissa sat across from a loan officer and signed a stack of papers that felt heavier than the house they were about to buy. They had spent years saving. They compared school districts. They drove past the property three times before making an offer. The down payment came from their savings account, built slowly from paychecks. That part made sense to them. Money saved. Money transferred.

The larger amount came from the bank.

Jacob imagined the source in simple terms. Somewhere, someone had deposited money. The bank gathered those deposits and lent a portion to them. He pictured a vault. Shelves. Ledgers. A quiet transfer from one pile to another.

The loan officer typed for a moment. A new number appeared in their account. Six figures. Instantly spendable. No other customer's balance moved down. No physical cash left a drawer. No vault opened.

A house was funded.

New money now existed in the economy that had not existed the day before. That quiet moment inside a small office captures something most people never pause to examine. Where did that money come from?

The common image many of us carry begins with printing presses and government mints. We learn that money is created by the state, printed, then distributed through the economy. It feels tangible. It feels controlled.

The historical record tells a more detailed story.

In 2014, the Bank of England published a paper titled "Money Creation in the Modern Economy." It explained, in plain language, that in modern banking systems, most money is created by commercial banks when they make loans.

The paper stated clearly: when a bank makes a loan, it creates a matching deposit in the borrower's account. That deposit is new money.

The authors were not offering a theory. They were describing standard accounting practice. To understand why this matters, we have to slow down and look at how bank balance sheets work.

When Jacob and Marissa signed their mortgage agreement, the bank added a new asset to its books: the mortgage contract, which promises repayment over time. At the same moment, the bank added a new liability: the deposit credited to their account. The deposit did not move from someone else's savings. It was created through an accounting entry. The loan created the deposit.

From the perspective of the broader economy, the money supply increased at that moment. A new deposit could now be spent. When Jacob and Marissa wired funds to the home seller, that deposit transferred into another account within the banking system. The money remained in circulation.

For many decades, economics textbooks described this process through what became known as the "money multiplier." In that simplified model, banks received deposits first and then lent out a portion while holding a required reserve. The size of the reserve requirement appeared to limit lending mechanically.

In March 2020, during the early days of the pandemic response, the Federal Reserve reduced reserve requirement ratios to zero percent. The change was announced as part of a broader effort to support credit flows. That moment clarified something important. In practice, banks extend loans based on capital requirements, risk assessment, and expected profitability. Reserves are managed afterward through the interbank market or central bank facilities. The order of operations matters. Lending creates deposits. Reserves support settlement.

This does not mean banks can create unlimited money without constraint. They operate within regulatory capital rules. They must meet liquidity standards. They face risk of loss if borrowers fail to repay. The system contains boundaries. Yet within those boundaries, new money enters the economy primarily through the act of lending.

Once that structure is understood, a deeper implication appears. When a bank creates a mortgage for Jacob and Marissa, it creates the principal amount of the loan. The contract specifies that over thirty years they will repay more than the principal. The additional amount is interest.

The principal is created at the moment of lending. The interest is scheduled to be paid from future income. That income may come from wages, business revenue, or other economic activity. Across the entire system, most money originates as loan principal. Interest obligations require ongoing income flows and, at a macro level, ongoing credit expansion to maintain liquidity.

This dynamic shapes the rhythm of the economy. When banks are confident and borrowers are eager, credit expands. Deposits increase. Money circulates. Construction firms hire workers. Home sellers receive funds. Spending spreads outward. Between 2000 and 2007, mortgage lending in the United States grew rapidly. Housing prices rose. Mortgage-backed securities expanded. Credit flowed easily. The growth of credit contributed to growth in broad money measures.

When credit freezes, money creation slows. When liquidity facilities are introduced, lending conditions improve. In 2023, after stress in regional banks following rising interest rates, the Federal Reserve introduced the Bank Term Funding Program. It allowed banks to borrow against high-quality collateral valued at par. The purpose was to prevent forced asset sales and maintain confidence in the banking system. The response reflected a consistent theme across decades: support the credit channel to preserve monetary stability.

At the level of lived experience, these mechanisms feel distant. Jacob and Marissa did not think about central bank balance sheets when they signed their mortgage. They felt relief. They felt possibility. They felt responsible for stepping into homeownership.

Over decades, as electronic payments and credit cards became common, societies adapted to debt as a routine tool. The act of borrowing blended into ordinary life. Few borrowers pause to consider that their loan has added new deposits to the banking system. They see a transaction. They see a monthly payment. The larger structural role remains invisible.

This invisibility carries consequences. When people believe money enters the economy primarily through printing presses, they imagine a fixed supply adjusted occasionally by government action. When they understand that money expands through credit relationships, they see a system that grows when balance sheets grow.

Money in this structure behaves differently from metal coin stored in vaults. It expands when loans are written. It contracts when loans are repaid or defaulted without replacement. The engine runs on credit. If the principal is created and interest obligations accumulate, the system depends on continuous economic activity and, often, further borrowing to maintain smooth functioning. This observation does not imply crisis at every turn. It describes a growth-oriented design. Modern economies aim for steady expansion in output, income, and credit.

When Jacob and Marissa make their monthly payment, part reduces principal. Part pays interest to the bank. The bank records income. The broader economy circulates funds through wages, profits, and taxes. At scale, millions of such transactions form the fabric of national income accounts.

The structure explains why lending conditions matter so much. It explains why policymakers focus intensely on credit markets during downturns. It explains why discussions of money creation revolve around banks and central banks rather than printing facilities.

Why Expansion Never Stops

If money enters the economy as debt with interest, the system inherits a quiet, structural requirement: the total amount owed always exceeds the principal created. This leads to structural tension. Payments of interest require income, which depends on economic activity, which depends on credit. When credit expands, spending expands; when it contracts, spending slows.

The Great Depression revealed this tension brutally. Between 1929 and 1933, bank failures wiped out deposits, shrinking credit and contracting the money supply by a third. Economic activity collapsed, leading to mass unemployment. The lesson was mechanical: the collapse of bank lending directly caused the collapse of the money supply, feeding a self-reinforcing contraction.

After reforms, the U.S. entered a long period of expanding credit, making growth embedded in economic planning. By the early 2000s, household debt climbed steadily, fueled by the housing finance boom. This expansion reversed between 2007 and 2009. Banks faced losses, and interbank lending froze. Policymakers, fearing another depression, responded aggressively. The Federal Reserve lowered rates to zero and began massive asset purchases - Quantitative Easing - expanding its balance sheet from under $1 trillion to over $4 trillion.

The objective was to stabilize credit and encourage lending, but the sequencing is telling. New credit and liquidity enter through financial institutions and capital markets first. Asset prices - owned disproportionately by the wealthy - recover quickly. The middle class, who depend on wage income, see their position erode. Housing prices stabilize, but the recovery in labor markets and wage growth lags for years.

This pattern repeated in 2020. The Fed again launched zero rates and large-scale asset purchases. The combined fiscal and monetary response caused broad money measures (M2) to surge at historically high rates. This rapid increase in spending power, meeting supply constraints, drove prices upward. The middle class was squeezed: asset owners saw portfolios rise, while wage earners faced rising rents and costs before their incomes could adjust proportionally. This staggered adjustment is a feature, not a bug, of the debt-based system, transferring wealth and risk.

In 2022 and 2023, rising interest rates introduced a new squeeze. As central banks raised rates, bond prices fell, creating hidden stress in banks. When stress appeared in regional banks in March 2023, the Federal Reserve intervened with facilities like the Bank Term Funding Program, ensuring liquidity for institutions. Across all these episodes, the pattern is consistent: when credit threatens to contract sharply, policymakers act to stabilize the system for the financial institutions at the core.

The system structurally leans toward expansion over long horizons, sustaining balance sheets. This structural reliance shapes the middle class's experience: they delay purchases when credit tightens and face inflation or rising asset costs during expansions. The economy appears to oscillate, with credit growth fueling investment and asset appreciation at the top, while contractions are managed to prevent a systemic collapse that would disproportionately impact financial institutions.

The deeper pattern is clear: money created through lending carries interest obligations, requiring continuous, credit-supported expansion. The tension is not merely behavioral; it arises from the arithmetic of debt combined with institutions designed to protect the flow of credit. When policy easing occurs, financial institutions and asset markets are the early recipients. The middle class, receiving income adjustments more gradually, pays the price during the contraction through lost jobs and during the expansion through rising cost of living that precedes rising wages. The engine continues turning, but the gears are designed to favor the few.

Who Stands Closest to the Source

Now that we have walked through how money is created and why expansion tends to continue, we can look at what that structure does over time.

Money creation is mechanical. Distribution is structural. The long-term effects show up slowly. They show up in housing prices, in asset markets, in retirement accounts, in the quiet pressure many households feel each month. They show up in who accumulates assets and who carries liabilities.

To see that clearly, we begin with government borrowing.

When a government spends more than it collects in taxes, it runs a deficit. To fund that deficit, it issues bonds. Those bonds are purchased by financial institutions, pension funds, insurance companies, foreign governments, and sometimes central banks through open market operations.

A bond is a promise to repay principal with interest. When investors purchase government bonds, funds are transferred to the Treasury. The government then spends those funds into the economy through salaries, contracts, benefits, and public programs.

From a structural perspective, this process matters because governments have continuous access to capital markets. Investors treat sovereign debt differently from household debt. Sovereign borrowers issue currency, collect taxes, and possess legal authority to structure repayment conditions.

This access changes the timing of consequences. An individual who overspends must either increase income, reduce spending, refinance, or default. A government that overspends can roll over its debt by issuing new bonds. As long as investors maintain confidence and central bank policy supports orderly markets, deficits can continue.

Over the past several decades, many developed nations have seen sustained increases in sovereign debt relative to GDP. The United States, for example, experienced large deficits during the financial crisis of 2008–2009 and again during the pandemic response in 2020–2021. Government debt levels rose accordingly.

This does not mean collapse is imminent. It does mean that debt expansion at the sovereign level becomes normalized within a credit-based system. When central banks purchase government securities during periods of stress, they support liquidity in bond markets. These purchases increase reserve balances in the banking system. The spending funded by those bonds enters the economy before tax adjustments occur. Over time, if spending expands faster than productive capacity, price levels adjust.

This is how inflation diffuses cost. It spreads the burden across currency holders gradually rather than through an immediate tax bill. The key structural difference between governments and individuals is access. Governments operate near the center of money creation channels. Individuals operate at the receiving end.

That positional difference compounds over time.

Consider the period after 2008. As the Federal Reserve expanded its balance sheet through asset purchases, financial conditions eased. Interest rates fell across maturities. Investors searching for yield moved into equities, corporate bonds, and real estate. Equity markets recovered strongly from their crisis lows. Over the following decade, major stock indices reached new highs. Housing prices, after stabilizing, resumed upward trajectories in many regions.

Wage growth also recovered, though at a more gradual pace. Labor markets improved steadily, yet the appreciation of financial assets outpaced median wage growth over much of that period. This sequencing follows transmission channels.

When central banks lower rates or purchase securities, financial institutions and investors adjust portfolios immediately. Asset valuations reflect discounted future cash flows. Lower discount rates increase present values. Prices respond. Wages depend on productivity, labor supply, contract negotiations, and business revenue growth. Those adjustments unfold over time.

The result is a structural pattern. Those who hold appreciating assets experience balance sheet gains early in expansion cycles. Those whose primary income derives from wages experience improvement later.

This pattern does not depend on intention. It depends on mechanism.

Over multiple cycles, early positioning compounds. If an investor owns real estate during a period of low interest rates, rising asset values increase equity. That equity can be used as collateral for additional borrowing. Additional borrowing can fund further investment. The balance sheet grows.

If a household holds primarily cash savings during the same period, purchasing power depends on wage growth relative to price growth. When asset prices rise faster than wages, entry becomes more expensive. Over time, this divergence affects wealth distribution.

Money creation involves two key actors: commercial banks and central banks.

Commercial banks decide who receives loans. They evaluate creditworthiness, collateral, income stability, and regulatory capital requirements. Central banks influence the cost of borrowing through policy rates and liquidity operations.

Access to credit depends on risk assessment and asset ownership. Large corporations with stable cash flows and collateral can borrow at relatively low rates. Governments borrow at lower rates still. Financial institutions borrow at interbank rates influenced directly by central bank policy.

Households borrow at rates that incorporate personal risk profiles. Credit cards carry higher rates than mortgages because they lack collateral and carry greater default risk. Small businesses often face higher borrowing costs than large corporations for similar reasons.

This layered structure creates differences in leverage capacity.

Those with lower borrowing costs can deploy capital more efficiently. When borrowing costs are below the expected return on investment, leverage amplifies gains. When borrowing costs exceed returns, leverage amplifies losses.

Over time, consistent access to lower-cost credit enables accumulation.

This pattern becomes visible when examining corporate behavior. Large firms often issue bonds at favorable rates to fund acquisitions or share buybacks. Asset prices respond to these capital flows. Shareholders benefit from appreciation and dividends.

Households with limited collateral rely more heavily on consumer credit. Higher interest payments reduce disposable income. The direction of leverage matters.

This structural hierarchy shapes lived experience.

If you rely primarily on wage income and modest savings, you experience the system differently from someone whose income derives from asset ownership.

During expansion phases, asset values rise. Housing prices increase. Rent follows. Entry into ownership becomes more difficult for first-time buyers.

Education costs, healthcare costs, and insurance premiums often rise with broader economic expansion. These costs interact with household budgets directly.

When inflation accelerates, central banks raise interest rates to slow credit growth. Mortgage rates increase. Auto loan rates increase. Credit card rates increase. Households carrying variable-rate debt feel the adjustment quickly. Asset holders may experience valuation declines in interest-rate-sensitive markets during tightening cycles. Yet those with diversified portfolios and access to credit often have flexibility to adjust.

The middle-income household often faces a narrower margin. Rising prices pressure budgets. Higher borrowing costs limit refinancing options. Wage adjustments occur gradually. The sensation that the finish line keeps moving arises from this structural dynamic. It reflects timing and positioning within the credit system.

Wealth concentration emerges through repeated cycles of expansion, leverage, and asset appreciation. Each cycle reinforces balance sheets that already contain appreciating assets. This pattern can be observed in wealth distribution data across many developed economies over recent decades. A growing share of total wealth is held by households owning financial assets and real estate. Wage income remains central for most households, yet asset appreciation plays a significant role in net worth growth.

The mechanism remains consistent with what we explored earlier. Money created through lending enters specific channels first. Those channels influence asset prices. Asset ownership shapes exposure to appreciation.

Over many decades, the global economy has evolved into a deeply financialized structure. Financial assets represent claims on future income streams. Credit connects present spending to future earnings. As debt levels rise relative to income across sectors, sensitivity to interest rate changes increases. Small shifts in rates can influence large pools of outstanding debt. Policymakers therefore weigh rate decisions carefully, balancing inflation control with financial stability.

This environment reinforces the importance of access to favorable credit terms. Those who borrow cheaply during expansion phases can accumulate assets more rapidly. Those who borrow expensively or remain entirely outside asset markets experience slower balance sheet growth.

The difference compounds over time. Money creation explains inflation. Inflation influences asset prices. Asset ownership shapes wealth accumulation. Wealth accumulation influences access to future credit.

The loop continues.

At this point, you can see the chain.

- Money enters the system through lending.
- Lending expands balance sheets.
- Balance sheet expansion influences asset values.
- Asset ownership influences wealth growth.
- Wealth influences access to future credit.

If you feel pressure while working steadily, the explanation rests in structure and timing. You stand at a particular point in the flow of money. That location shapes outcomes.

Understanding this structure encourages you to examine your balance sheet alongside your income statement. It encourages you to consider how credit cycles affect your plans. It encourages you to think in terms of positioning rather than effort alone.

You cannot change the structure of money creation on your own. You can change how you position yourself within it.

As we move forward, one layer remains to explore.

Not all debt costs the same. Not all borrowers receive equal terms. The price of money depends on proximity to its source.

Understanding that difference opens the next chapter.

CHAPTER 6

WHO GETS THE CHEAP MONEY?

On a Thursday morning in the summer of 2020, Johnson sat at his kitchen table with his laptop open and his coffee going cold.

The news banner across the screen read: **"Interest Rates Fall to Historic Lows."**

The article explained that the 10-year U.S. Treasury yield had dropped below 1 percent. Commentators called it extraordinary. Borrowing, they said, had become cheaper than anyone could remember.

Johnson felt a flicker of relief. He and his wife had been trying to refinance their mortgage. They carried a balance on a credit card from a recent medical bill. Their car loan still had three years left. If money was suddenly cheap, perhaps this was their moment. Later that afternoon, his credit card statement arrived. The interest rate printed at the top was 22.4 percent. His refinance quote came in slightly lower than before, though closing costs had risen. The auto loan offer from another bank looked almost identical to the old one.

Johnson felt confused.

If rates were falling everywhere, why did nothing feel cheaper?

Interest rates are presented as universal. The headlines say rates are up or rates are down, as if everyone experiences the same conditions. They do not. The cost of money depends on your position in the system.

That idea sounds abstract at first. It becomes clearer when we step back and look at what was happening in 2020.

In early 2020, as the pandemic spread, investors around the world sought safety. They bought U.S. Treasury bonds in large volumes. When demand for bonds rises, yields fall. At the same time, the Federal Reserve lowered its policy rate and began purchasing large amounts of Treasury securities and mortgage-backed securities. These actions increased demand further and pushed yields lower still.

By the summer of 2020, the yield on the 10-year Treasury had fallen below 1 percent. For the U.S. government, this mattered. Treasury yields represent the interest rate the government pays to borrow money for ten years. When yields fall, the government can issue new debt at lower cost. It can refinance existing obligations more cheaply. Large institutional investors also use Treasury yields as a benchmark for pricing many other forms of debt.

From the government's perspective, money had become very inexpensive. Yet during that same period, the average interest rate on credit cards remained in the mid-to-high teens, and in many cases above 20 percent. Auto loan rates varied widely depending on credit score and term. Personal loans often carried double-digit rates. Mortgage rates did decline, though access depended on credit history, income stability, and property valuation.

The difference between a Treasury yield below 1 percent and a credit card rate above 20 percent is not a rounding error. It reflects a structural hierarchy.

- At the top sits the sovereign borrower: the U.S. government. Its debt is considered among the safest assets in the world. It controls taxation authority. It issues bonds in its own currency. Demand for its securities is deep and global.
- Below the government sit large financial institutions. They fund themselves in part through deposits and in part through wholesale markets. They also have access to central bank facilities.
- Corporations with strong balance sheets and investment-grade credit ratings follow. They issue bonds priced relative to Treasury yields, plus a spread that reflects perceived risk.
- Small businesses often rely on bank loans or credit lines. Pricing reflects their cash flow, collateral, and industry risk.
- Workers and households sit at the end of this chain. They borrow through mortgages, auto loans, credit cards, student loans, or personal loans. Pricing reflects income stability, credit history, and whether the loan is secured by collateral.

Government. Banks. Corporations. Small businesses. Workers.

By the time money reaches the average household, it is expensive.

To understand Johnson's confusion, we need to separate two ideas that often blend together in public conversation: policy rates and consumer rates.

When the Federal Reserve lowers its target federal funds rate, it changes the rate at which banks lend reserves to one another overnight. This is a foundational rate in the banking system. It influences short-term funding costs. It sends a signal about monetary policy. It affects financial conditions broadly.

Yet the federal funds rate is not the rate printed on Johnson's credit card statement.

Banks also have access to the Federal Reserve's discount window. Through this facility, they can borrow directly from the central bank against approved collateral at a stated rate. During periods of stress, the Federal Reserve has created additional programs. In 2008, it established the Primary Dealer Credit Facility to lend to large broker-dealers that serve as intermediaries in government securities markets. In 2020, it launched corporate credit facilities to support bond markets and help stabilize funding for large employers.

These facilities operate at the institutional level. They aim to maintain liquidity in key markets. They are designed to prevent funding freezes that can ripple through the financial system.

Money, in these moments, enters through institutions.

It flows outward.

As it moves further from the center, its price changes.

This does not mean that policymakers set high rates for households and low rates for governments as a matter of preference. It means that the structure of the system places different borrowers at different distances from the source of liquidity.

Governments issue bonds directly into deep capital markets. Large institutions interact with the central bank. Corporations issue debt through underwriters who price bonds relative to benchmark yields. Households rely on retail lending channels where pricing incorporates administrative costs, default risk, and profit margins.

Each step adds layers.

Each layer has a price.

When lenders price a loan, they consider several factors: the likelihood of repayment, the presence of collateral, the duration of the loan, and the broader economic environment.

- A U.S. Treasury bond is backed by the full faith and credit of the United States government. It trades in vast volumes every day. Investors around the world treat it as a benchmark for safety.
- A mortgage loan is backed by a house. If the borrower defaults, the lender has a claim on the property. The rate reflects both the borrower's credit profile and the value of the collateral.
- A credit card balance is unsecured. The lender's claim rests primarily on the borrower's future income and credit history. The rate compensates for the higher probability of missed payments and the lack of tangible collateral.

From a lender's perspective, these differences justify different prices.

From Johnson's perspective, the headline "Rates Are Down" created an expectation that did not align with his lived experience.

Here is where psychology enters.

Researchers in behavioral economics describe a concept known as anchoring. When people hear a number, especially a number repeated in media, they tend to use it as a reference point for related judgments. If the news says "rates are near zero," that number becomes an anchor. It shapes expectations. There is also a form of distance bias at work. Central bank policy feels abstract. Treasury yields feel technical. Most people interact with money through bills, statements, and loan offers. When a single rate is discussed publicly, it feels as though it should apply universally.

When you hear "rates are low," you assume it applies to you.

Yet the financial system is layered. The headline rate reflects conditions near the top of the hierarchy. As money travels downward through institutions, underwriting standards, and retail channels, its price shifts.

This pattern has repeated across crises and recoveries.

In 2008, as credit markets froze, the Federal Reserve created facilities to support primary dealers and securitized lending markets. In 2020, as markets convulsed, similar programs were revived and expanded. Each time, the goal was to stabilize the plumbing of the financial system. Asset prices often responded quickly. Equity markets recovered. Bond spreads narrowed.

Labor markets and household balance sheets adjusted more slowly.

This sequence follows from structure rather than intent.

Money is introduced or supported at the institutional level first. It reaches households through secondary channels.

By the time it arrives, it carries a different price.

Consider again the hierarchy:

- Governments borrow at the lowest rates.
- Large financial institutions borrow just above that.
- Corporations with assets and influence follow.
- Small businesses come next.
- Workers come last.

Each rung on this ladder reflects access to collateral, scale, and proximity to capital markets.

Johnson's 22.4 percent credit card rate reflects his position on that ladder. It incorporates statistical models of default risk. It accounts for unsecured exposure. It includes servicing costs and profit margins.

The Treasury's sub-1 percent yield reflects global demand for safe assets, central bank purchases, and the government's taxing authority.

Both rates exist within the same monetary system.

They are simply attached to different positions within it. Not all money is created equal. And not everyone pays the same price for it. This is the part of the system most people never see.

When money was described as "cheap" in 2020, it was cheap at the top of the ladder. As it moved downward, it acquired layers of risk pricing and intermediation.

By the time it reached Johnson's mailbox, it felt expensive. If money were truly cheap in a universal sense, his emergency would cost very little to finance. The fact that it did not tells us something about structure.

This is not accidental.

It is structural.

Who Gets the Money Before Prices Move

In September of 2008, credit markets stopped trusting one another.

Large financial institutions, which normally lent freely to each other overnight, began to hesitate. Funding markets tightened. Firms that relied on short-term borrowing faced uncertainty. The collapse of Lehman Brothers intensified that uncertainty. What had been a steady flow of credit became cautious and selective.

The Federal Reserve responded in stages. First, it lowered its policy rate. Then it introduced new facilities designed to restore liquidity to specific corners of the financial system. Among them was the Primary Dealer Credit Facility, which allowed major securities dealers to borrow against collateral. Soon after, the Term Asset-Backed Securities Loan Facility was created to support the issuance of highly rated asset-backed securities. In November 2008, the Federal Reserve announced large-scale purchases of mortgage-backed securities and Treasury bonds, an initiative later referred to as quantitative easing, or QE1.

Each program had a defined purpose. The aim was to stabilize markets that serve as the backbone of modern finance. Mortgage-backed securities markets influence housing finance. Treasury markets anchor global pricing. Primary dealers facilitate trading and liquidity in government bonds. When these areas function smoothly, credit flows more predictably throughout the economy.

The design of these interventions reveals something important about order.

Liquidity entered at the institutional level first.

Primary dealers could borrow through the new facilities. Banks holding mortgage-backed securities could sell them into a central bank purchase program. Investors in AAA-rated asset-backed securities could access funding through TALF. These measures lowered yields on targeted assets and restored confidence in specific funding channels.

Asset prices responded relatively quickly. Equity markets began to stabilize in 2009. Credit spreads narrowed. Bond issuance resumed. Capital markets reopened.

Labor markets adjusted more slowly. Unemployment in the United States rose to 10 percent in October 2009. Wage growth remained subdued for years. The stabilization of financial markets preceded the recovery of household income.

This sequence follows from structure. The tools available to policymakers operate through financial institutions and markets. The transmission to wages and household cash flow depends on hiring decisions, business investment, and consumer demand, all of which move with delay.

Those closest to money creation receive new money before prices adjust.

They borrow cheaply.

They deploy capital into assets.

They benefit from appreciation driven by expansion.

To see how this becomes self-reinforcing, consider the mechanics step by step.

When the Federal Reserve purchases large quantities of Treasury bonds or mortgage-backed securities, it increases demand for those assets. Increased demand raises prices. Bond prices and yields move in opposite directions, so as prices rise, yields fall. Lower yields reduce borrowing costs for governments and, indirectly, for corporations whose debt is priced relative to those benchmarks.

Lower yields make existing bonds with higher coupons more valuable. Investors holding those assets experience gains. Portfolio managers rebalance into other securities, often moving into corporate bonds, equities, or real estate investment trusts in search of return. This portfolio shift supports asset prices more broadly.

Cheap money buys assets.

Assets rise in price.

Rising asset prices increase the value of collateral held by banks, corporations, and investors. Higher collateral values improve balance sheets. Improved balance sheets make additional borrowing easier. Lenders feel more comfortable extending credit when the underlying assets have appreciated.

Assets are used as collateral.

Collateral unlocks more cheap money.

This compounding loop does not require dramatic assumptions. It follows from basic lending practice. A bank that sees a borrower's asset base increase may extend a larger line of credit. An investor who sees the value of a portfolio rise can borrow against it at favorable rates. A corporation whose bond yields have declined can refinance existing debt at lower cost and issue new debt to fund acquisitions or share buybacks.

During the years following the 2008 crisis, U.S. corporate bond issuance expanded significantly. Many large firms refinanced debt at lower rates. Equity markets experienced one of the longest bull runs in modern history. Household net worth, particularly among those holding financial assets, recovered and grew.

This does not imply that central bank policy alone created these outcomes. Technological change, globalization, fiscal policy, and demographic trends also shaped the recovery. Yet the order in which liquidity entered the system influenced who could respond first.

The idea sometimes referred to as the "Fed put" emerged during this period. The term describes a market belief that central banks will ease policy or provide liquidity when asset prices fall sharply. The phrase traces back to commentary during the tenure of Federal Reserve Chair Alan Greenspan, particularly after the stock market crash of October 1987 and subsequent episodes of easing.

Beliefs shape behavior. When investors expect that severe market declines will be met with policy support, perceived downside risk shifts. Portfolio managers may accept higher valuations or greater leverage when they assume that liquidity will return in times of stress. This expectation does not eliminate risk. It changes how risk is weighed.

Meanwhile, households operate under different constraints.

Expensive debt creates pressure. A household carrying high-interest credit card balances may focus on minimum payments and immediate cash flow. The compounding nature of interest works against them. Opportunities to invest or accumulate assets feel distant when current obligations demand attention.

Institutions with appreciating collateral experience the opposite psychological environment. Rising asset values expand perceived options. Access to low-cost credit increases flexibility. Strategic decisions can be made with longer horizons.

This asymmetry in mindset compounds the asymmetry in pricing.

A historical example illustrates how systemic risk is treated differently from individual risk.

In 1998, Long-Term Capital Management, a hedge fund employing significant leverage, faced severe losses during the Russian financial crisis. Its positions were large relative to market liquidity. Concern grew that a disorderly liquidation could destabilize financial markets. The Federal Reserve Bank of New York facilitated discussions among major financial institutions, leading to a private-sector recapitalization of the fund. The goal was to prevent contagion.

The rescue did not absolve investors of losses. It aimed to contain systemic fallout.

Contrast this with an individual who misses a credit card payment. The penalty is immediate. Late fees apply. Interest rates may increase. Credit scores decline. Access to future borrowing becomes more expensive.

- Losses at the top are absorbed through coordinated measures when systemic stability is at stake.
- Losses at the bottom are punished through contractual terms designed to manage individual credit risk.

Both responses follow from structure. A large hedge fund with interconnected positions poses potential spillover effects. A single household default does not threaten market plumbing.

The distinction shapes outcomes.

During the 2020 crisis, similar patterns emerged. The Federal Reserve established corporate credit facilities to support bond markets. Treasury yields fell sharply as investors sought safety and as central bank purchases expanded. Investment-grade corporations issued record amounts of debt at historically low rates. Many refinanced obligations and extended maturities.

At the same time, small businesses navigated uncertainty through programs such as the Paycheck Protection Program, which offered government-backed loans at low stated rates with forgiveness provisions tied to payroll maintenance. Access varied depending on banking relationships and administrative capacity. Households received direct fiscal support, yet consumer credit pricing remained differentiated by credit profile and collateral.

Markets recovered quickly after March 2020. Major equity indices reached new highs within months. Employment levels took longer to normalize.

This sequence reflects the order of liquidity transmission. By the time inflation shows up in everyday life, the advantage has already been captured. When asset prices rise first, those holding assets experience gains. When borrowing costs decline first for large issuers, they can refinance and invest before broader price adjustments occur. When wages adjust later, purchasing power may already face pressure from higher asset valuations, including housing.

Large institutions expand during periods of monetary easing while households navigate higher asset prices and tighter lending standards.

- This advantage compounds.
- Cheap money buys assets.
- Assets rise in price.
- Assets are used as collateral.
- Collateral unlocks more cheap money.
- Over time, wealth concentrates among those positioned to participate in this loop.

Workers are not viewed as low-risk borrowers in the same way as asset-rich institutions. Their primary collateral is future income. Income can fluctuate with employment conditions. Lenders price this uncertainty. Interest rates reflect statistical models built on credit histories and income stability.

A missed payment triggers automatic adjustments. Contracts specify consequences. Credit scores serve as a summary measure of past repayment behavior. Access can shrink quickly when payments lapse. There is no broad facility designed to stabilize an individual's credit card balance in a downturn. There are hardship programs and restructuring options, yet these operate within retail banking frameworks rather than through systemic liquidity tools.

The structure that forgives institutional losses in order to protect market functioning enforces individual discipline through contract terms and credit scoring.

The tension here builds from mechanics rather than emotion.

If you had access to 1 percent money backed by appreciating assets, how would you use it?

You might acquire more assets. You might refinance existing obligations. You might extend your horizon and take calculated risks.

If your borrowing costs sit above 20 percent and your collateral consists primarily of wages, your decisions will look different. You may prioritize immediate repayment. You may avoid long-term commitments. You may defer investment.

The real divider is leverage.

Leverage refers to borrowing against assets with the expectation that the return on those assets will exceed the cost of debt. When leverage is paired with appreciating collateral and low borrowing costs, it can amplify gains. When leverage is paired with unstable income and high interest rates, it can amplify stress.

The financial system channels cheap money toward those with collateral and scale. That channel shapes asset prices, borrowing capacity, and behavioral incentives.

Leverage Is the Divider

Leverage is simply the use of borrowed money to control assets. It can magnify gains. It can magnify losses. Its impact depends on cost, collateral, and discipline.

When someone borrows at 3 percent to purchase an asset that yields 6 percent, the spread between cost and return works in their favor. When someone borrows at 20 percent to cover consumption, the spread works against them.

- Debt used for consumption is expensive.
- Debt used for assets can be structured to compound.

Over long periods, small differences in borrowing costs produce large differences in outcomes. A corporation that refinances billions of dollars at lower rates reduces interest expense significantly. Those savings can be reinvested, used to acquire competitors, or returned to shareholders. An investor who borrows at low rates to purchase appreciating assets increases exposure to growth.

Meanwhile, a household carrying high-interest balances allocates income toward servicing debt. The opportunity cost accumulates quietly.

Over decades, these patterns shape wealth distribution.

Data from the Federal Reserve's Survey of Consumer Finances shows that financial assets are concentrated among higher-income households. When asset prices rise, those holding them benefit disproportionately. When borrowing costs decline for investment-grade issuers, they can expand balance sheets efficiently.

Middle-income households often hold wealth primarily in their primary residence and retirement accounts. Lower-income households hold little in financial assets and rely more heavily on wage income. When housing prices rise, entry becomes harder for new buyers. When equity markets surge, those without exposure see little direct benefit. When consumer credit rates remain elevated, debt servicing absorbs income.

The pressure on the middle class emerges from this structure. It feels like standing on a moving walkway that shifts speed depending on your footing. Those with assets find the walkway moving with them. Those relying solely on wages must walk faster to keep pace.

You have likely felt this in subtle ways.

You may have noticed housing prices rising faster than your salary. You may have seen stock market indices reach new highs while your savings account earns little. You may have wondered why borrowing for education or emergencies carries a cost far above the rates discussed in policy meetings.

These experiences connect structural economics to daily life. People sense imbalance. They see corporations buying back shares during periods of low interest rates. They see governments issuing large amounts of debt at manageable yields. They see banks reporting profits after crises.

At the same time, households are encouraged to budget carefully, build emergency funds, and avoid unnecessary debt.

Both sets of advice operate within the same system. The rules are consistent. They are not equal.

The system protects those whose failure would disrupt markets. It disciplines individual borrowers through contract terms and credit scoring.

Access determines cost. Cost determines outcome. The system rewards ownership because ownership provides collateral. Collateral lowers borrowing costs. Lower borrowing costs expand options. Labor remains essential. It produces income. It builds skill. It supports families. Yet within a debt-based system, labor alone sits farther from the source of cheap money than asset ownership does.

That distance influences compounding.

Consider two individuals at age thirty.

One carries student loans at moderate rates and begins investing early, acquiring diversified assets over time. As their portfolio grows, they gain access to lower-cost borrowing secured by those assets. They refinance obligations when possible. They think in decades.

The other carries revolving consumer debt at high rates and rents in a market with rising housing costs. Their income covers necessities with little margin. Investment feels distant. Borrowing remains expensive.

Both may work equally hard.

Their positions differ.

Over thirty years, those differences compound.

Johnson, at his kitchen table, was not foolish. He was far from the source of cheap money. His credit card rate reflected his place in the hierarchy. His confusion arose from hearing a headline that described conditions at the top of the system while he operated at the bottom.

Once he understands that distinction, his frustration becomes information.

- Cheap money explains who wins.
- Expensive money explains who struggles.
- Leverage explains the divide.
- Position explains the outcome.

Yet there is one more layer beneath this. Debt does more than price risk. It shapes behavior. It influences choices. It creates habits of caution or expansion. It builds dependence when obligations crowd out options.

To understand why people remain in positions that limit them, even when they see the system clearly, we must look at how debt molds psychology over time.

CHAPTER 7

DEBT CONTROL

Adam wakes up at 6:15 every morning. His day has a shape, and that shape is built around dates. The first of the month matters. The fifteenth matters. The twenty-second matters. He knows which bills clear automatically and which require a manual click. His mortgage drafts on the first. His student loan withdraws on the fifteenth. His credit card minimum posts on the twenty-second. His car payment sits in between.

Adam earns a steady salary. He owns a modest home. He drives a reliable car. He has never missed a payment. Nothing about his finances looks reckless. Nothing looks extreme. He once talked about starting a small consulting business. He once thought about moving to a different state. He once considered taking six months off after his second child was born. Those conversations still sit somewhere in his memory. They surface sometimes when he drives to work.

Then he thinks about the first. The fifteenth. The twenty-second.

Have you ever noticed how bold ideas feel different when your bills are already scheduled?

Adam is not physically constrained. No one stands in his doorway telling him where to go. He is free in a legal sense. Yet his options feel narrow. A missed paycheck would ripple instantly through his calendar. His mortgage company would not wait. His loan servicer would not adjust its schedule to match his curiosity. The credit card company would add a late fee and adjust his interest rate.

Debt limits choices, not freedom of movement. When choices narrow, behavior becomes predictable.

Adam stays in a job he does not love because the bills must be paid. His employer offers health insurance, steady income, and predictable hours. The predictability matters. Risk feels expensive. A missed payment carries a cost that compounds quickly. Fear of missing payments shapes his decision-making more than ambition does.

This creates a quiet agreement. "I will behave today to avoid pain tomorrow." That sentence is rarely spoken out loud. It lives inside the calendar. It lives inside the autopay settings. It lives inside the steady hum of low-grade stress that becomes normal over time.

Even when income rises, the anxiety remains. A promotion increases pay. It also increases lifestyle commitments. A larger home. A longer mortgage. A higher property tax bill. The margin for error remains thin. The structure stays intact.

Adam is not weak. He is responding rationally to a system built around scheduled obligation.

To understand how this structure became ordinary, we have to step back nearly a century.

In October 1929, stock prices collapsed. The decline did not end in a single week. It unfolded across months and years. Banks failed in waves between 1930 and 1933. Depositors lost savings. Businesses closed. Unemployment climbed above 20 percent by 1933. Many households that believed they were secure found themselves without income and without access to their own deposits.

Before this period, many home loans were short-term and structured differently than they are today. A common mortgage in the 1920s required a large down payment, often 50 percent, and lasted five years or less. Borrowers paid interest during the term and then faced a large balloon payment at the end. If they could not refinance, they lost the property. When banks failed and credit tightened during the early 1930s, refinancing became difficult. Foreclosures increased sharply.

The crisis did more than reduce wealth. It changed how people thought about safety. Families who lived through bank failures developed a deep preference for stability. Income that arrived consistently mattered more than income that fluctuated. Cash on hand mattered more than future potential.

Policymakers responded with structural reforms designed to stabilize the housing market and the banking system. In 1933, the federal government created the Home Owners' Loan Corporation to refinance distressed mortgages. In 1934, Congress established the Federal Housing Administration. The FHA did not lend directly. It insured mortgages issued by private lenders. If a borrower defaulted, the federal government absorbed part of the loss.

This insurance changed incentives. Lenders faced lower risk. They could extend longer loan terms. The 30-year amortizing mortgage became standard over time. Instead of a five-year loan with a balloon payment, borrowers could spread repayment across three decades. Each payment included both principal and interest. By the end of the term, the loan would be fully repaid.

The financial mechanism was simple. A longer loan term reduces the size of each monthly payment. Lower monthly payments allow more households to qualify. Broader participation supports home construction and related industries. Stability increases.

Longer term → Smaller monthly payment → Broader access → Decades-long obligation.

The policy goal was stabilization. The behavioral consequence was normalization of long-term debt. Security became the reward. Predictability became the requirement.

When a household signs a 30-year mortgage, it makes a promise about future income. The lender assesses current earnings, but the loan assumes that income will continue for decades. The monthly payment anchors future labor. A household that owes 360 payments has a strong incentive to preserve steady employment.

After World War II, another policy expanded this structure. The Servicemen's Readjustment Act of 1944, widely known as the GI Bill, provided loan guarantees for returning veterans. Millions of families gained access to home financing with low down payments and favorable terms. Homeownership rose sharply in the postwar decades. Suburban development expanded. The middle class grew in size and stability.

These programs increased access. They supported wealth-building through property ownership. They also embedded long-term repayment schedules into ordinary life. A mortgage became part of adulthood. It signaled responsibility. It signaled arrival.

As consumer credit markets developed after the war, installment plans became common for appliances and automobiles. A refrigerator could be purchased with a down payment and monthly installments. A car could be financed across several years. Instead of saving the full amount in advance, households could borrow against future income.

Borrowing against the future spreads cost over time. It also spreads obligation over time. When a payment is due every month, attention shifts toward maintaining the income that supports it. A worker considering a career change calculates risk differently when fixed payments exist. The more payments scheduled, the narrower the margin for experimentation.

This pattern deepened as credit markets matured. In the 1950s and 1960s, banks and finance companies expanded consumer lending. By the late twentieth century, revolving credit through credit cards allowed households to carry balances indefinitely, paying interest in exchange for flexibility.

Each step made participation easier. Each step tied present choices to future payments.

Fear of missing payments overrides long-term thinking because the consequences are immediate. Late fees apply quickly. Interest compounds. Credit records reflect delinquency. The structure does not need force to operate. It operates through contract and calendar.

Over time, this creates a background level of stress. The stress does not always feel dramatic. It feels steady. It becomes normal. A household may increase income, yet expenses rise alongside it. A larger home carries higher maintenance costs and property taxes. A new car replaces an old one with a new loan term. Obligations refresh themselves.

People adapt. They budget. They schedule. They comply with the rhythm of repayment.

This is the silent contract of debt-based living. I will behave today to avoid pain tomorrow.

The shift from a world where labor was traded primarily for tangible goods into one where labor services ongoing debt did not occur overnight. It unfolded across decades through policy changes, financial innovation, and cultural reinforcement. The Great Depression created a demand for security. Federal mortgage insurance and loan guarantees met that demand. Installment credit and long-term financing spread the model across goods and services.

The system achieved many of its stated goals. It stabilized housing markets. It broadened access to ownership. It supported economic growth.

It also reshaped psychology. When obligations stretch across decades, freedom feels abstract and payments feel concrete. When risk carries the possibility of default, stability carries emotional weight.

Return to Adam.

He lives inside a structure built long before he was born. His mortgage resembles the standardized form introduced in the 1930s. His expectation of stable employment echoes the lessons learned during the Great Depression. His comfort with installment payments reflects decades of consumer credit expansion.

He wakes at 6:15. He checks his calendar. He drives to work.

He is not trapped by visible chains. He is anchored by scheduled promises.

Debt, in this form, shapes behavior quietly. It narrows options through obligation. It encourages compliance through predictability. It trains households to prioritize certainty over experimentation.

The worker is not flawed. He is rational within the system he inhabits.

And that system began with a promise: stability in exchange for structured repayment.

The Legal Expansion of Consumer Credit

You might think the mortgage was the end of the story. It was only the beginning. In the decades after the Second World War, debt became common. By the 1960s, installment loans financed cars and appliances across the country. By the 1970s, bank credit cards were spreading nationally. Monthly payments were no longer unusual. They were routine.

Then something subtle changed. Debt stopped being just a private agreement between borrower and lender. It became data. And once debt becomes data, it becomes scalable.

Before the 1970s, local lenders often relied on informal information. A banker might know a borrower's family. A store owner might extend credit based on reputation. Records existed, but they were fragmented and inconsistent. Errors were common. Access to information varied widely across regions.

As consumer lending expanded, lenders wanted uniformity. They wanted to price risk more precisely. They wanted to decide quickly.

While reporting and scoring formalized borrower behavior, another shift altered the cost and reach of consumer credit. In 1978, the Supreme Court decided Marquette National Bank v. First of Omaha Service Corp. The Court held that national banks could charge interest rates allowed in the state where they were located, even when lending to customers in other states with lower rate caps.

The ruling had a clear legal basis. It interpreted existing banking law. Its economic consequence unfolded over the next decade.

Banks headquartered in states with higher permissible interest rates could extend credit cards nationally while applying those higher rates. Several states adjusted their regulations to attract financial institutions. Credit card lending expanded rapidly during the 1980s and 1990s. The financial mechanism here rests on pricing. Higher permissible rates make unsecured lending more profitable. Greater profitability supports broader marketing and looser qualification thresholds. Revolving credit becomes widely available.

Revolving credit differs from installment loans in one key way. Instead of a fixed schedule that amortizes the balance to zero over a set period, revolving credit allows the borrower to carry a balance indefinitely, as long as minimum payments are made.

- Minimum payments are small relative to total balances. They create short-term flexibility. They also extend repayment over long horizons when balances remain high.
- From a household perspective, this can feel manageable. A $2,000 balance may require a minimum payment of perhaps 2 to 3 percent. The immediate cash requirement appears modest.
- From a structural perspective, the math compounds. Interest accrues on the remaining balance. If only minimum payments are made, the principal declines slowly.
- People respond to immediate demands more strongly than distant ones. A small minimum payment relieves present pressure. The long-term interest cost feels abstract.
- Behavioral economists describe this as present bias. Immediate relief weighs more heavily in decision-making than distant cost.

- When credit cards became widely available under the new legal environment, borrowing for everyday expenses increased. Households gained flexibility. They also gained ongoing balances.

The system did not need to compel borrowing. It made borrowing convenient. Convenience shapes habits.

At this point, the structure reaches maturity. Debt exists. It is recorded. It is scored. It is priced dynamically. It is widely available.

What does this do to everyday conduct?

Imagine considering a job change that involves a temporary pay cut. If you carry a mortgage, auto loan, and revolving credit balance, your ability to absorb income variability depends on liquidity. If liquidity is thin, stability becomes attractive.

Imagine thinking about starting a business. Lenders may review your credit history before extending a small business loan. You may hesitate to risk a late payment during a transition period because it could lower your score and raise future borrowing costs.

Imagine facing an unexpected expense. You can use credit to manage it. The relief is immediate. The repayment schedule extends into the future.

Over time, the pattern becomes familiar. Scheduled obligations guide decisions. The credit file reinforces compliance. The score quantifies risk.

This creates what can be described as invisible discipline. There is no central authority directing individual life choices. There is a system of incentives and records that shape those choices indirectly. The constant low-grade stress becomes part of the background. Income rises across a career. So do obligations. Anxiety does not disappear. It adjusts to new thresholds.

Debt keeps attention anchored to upcoming payments and past performance. It narrows the field of perceived options. Indebted citizens become predictable in aggregate. They maintain employment to service obligations. They avoid actions that might disrupt income. They monitor their credit standing. Dependency feels familiar because it is structured into everyday routines. Certainty carries value when payments are fixed. Uncertainty carries cost when credit access matters.

The silent contract remains intact: ***I will behave today to avoid pain tomorrow***.

Debt now follows you across geography and across time. It influences housing, insurance, employment, and interest rates. Compliance rarely feels dramatic. It feels practical.

The structure operates through numbers and schedules.

Obligation and Concentration

By now, you can see the pattern forming.

Debt begins as access. It becomes obligation. It becomes data.

Over time, it becomes leverage. The long-term impact of this structure shows up in two places at once. It shows up in household decision-making. And it shows up in wealth distribution.

Let's start with something simple.

Not all debt carries the same flexibility.

In earlier decades of American law, bankruptcy functioned as a reset mechanism. It carried social stigma, yet it allowed certain debts to be discharged so that individuals could restart. Over time, specific categories of debt became more difficult to escape.

Student loans offer a clear example. Beginning in the 1970s and continuing through legislative changes in 1998 and 2005, Congress narrowed the circumstances under which federal and private student loans could be discharged in bankruptcy. Today, discharge generally requires proving "undue hardship," a legal standard that courts interpret narrowly.

The financial mechanism is straightforward. When a debt cannot easily be discharged, the lender's risk declines. When lender risk declines, access to capital expands. Student lending grew substantially across the 1990s and 2000s.

For the borrower, the experience feels different. A student loan follows you through career changes, relocations, and economic downturns. It adjusts to income in some programs. It accrues interest consistently. It remains present.

If your debt cannot easily disappear, how bold are you willing to be?

Debt relief rules shape risk tolerance. When obligations persist regardless of employment shifts, people gravitate toward stable income. Stability becomes a strategy for survival.

In 2005, the Bankruptcy Abuse Prevention and Consumer Protection Act tightened access to Chapter 7 liquidation bankruptcy and introduced additional requirements for filers. The law aimed to reduce perceived abuse of the system and to ensure that those with repayment capacity used structured repayment plans. Filing declined after its passage.

The mechanism matters. When legal exits narrow, obligations extend. When obligations extend, bargaining power shifts.

A worker considering a lower-paying opportunity must now calculate long-term repayment obligations that cannot be reset easily. A family weighing entrepreneurial risk must factor in debts that remain regardless of business outcomes.

Longer obligation → Lower risk tolerance → Reduced experimentation.

This sequence does not require moral framing. It flows from structure.

Over time, households orient toward preserving creditworthiness and stable income because the cost of disruption feels high. That orientation aggregates across millions of families.

Here is where structure becomes visible at scale.

- Debt explains compliance.
- Compliance explains stable labor supply.
- Stable labor supply supports steady production and consumption.
- Steady production and consumption support corporate earnings.
- Corporate earnings support asset prices.

This chain operates through incentives. When households maintain stable employment to service obligations, businesses benefit from reliable labor. When households continue making payments, banks receive predictable cash flows. When those cash flows are bundled into securities or reflected in earnings, investors price them accordingly.

Asset ownership sits closer to these cash flows. Consider the difference between two positions within the system. One household carries mortgage, auto, student loan, and credit card obligations. Its net worth may include home equity, yet much of its monthly income services debt. Its primary asset is labor.

Another household or institution owns shares in banks, real estate investment trusts, or diversified equity portfolios. It benefits from the interest paid by borrowers, the rent paid by tenants, and the earnings generated by firms employing stable labor.

When debt expands structurally and repayment remains consistent, financial assets tied to those repayments tend to appreciate over time, subject to cycles.

Those closest to low-cost capital can acquire appreciating assets more easily. Those anchored by high-cost consumer debt devote more of their income to servicing past purchases.

Over decades, this difference compounds. Wealth concentration emerges from compounding ownership of appreciating assets, supported by stable repayment streams across the broader population. Middle-class pressure emerges from balancing income growth against expanding obligations.

You may notice a shift in how participation feels.

Earlier in the century, ownership often required accumulated savings before purchase. Over time, borrowing enabled earlier access. That access expanded opportunity. It also introduced ongoing management of debt. Participation in modern economic life often means managing credit, monitoring scores, refinancing loans, adjusting payment schedules, and responding to rate changes.

This is managed participation.

You participate in housing markets through mortgages. You participate in education through student loans. You participate in consumption through credit cards. You participate in retirement markets through payroll deductions and investment accounts.

Each layer requires attention. Each layer requires income continuity.

Ownership still exists. Many households build equity and savings over time. Yet ownership often coexists with leverage. The structural difference lies in who primarily owns income-producing assets and who primarily services obligations. Those who own diversified portfolios benefit from appreciation linked to broad economic activity. Those who rely primarily on wages and carry substantial debt remain sensitive to employment stability and interest rates.

This creates a steady upward pull on asset values and a steady downward pressure on discretionary income for heavily indebted households.

Over time, the gap widens.

So, what does this mean for you?

1. Debt itself is a tool. It can finance education, housing, and enterprise. It can accelerate opportunity when aligned with productive assets.
2. Unconscious debt reduces optionality. When obligations consume most of your cash flow, your ability to pivot shrinks. Your risk tolerance contracts.
3. Understanding structure restores perspective. If you feel pressure to maintain stability at all costs, recognize the incentives shaping that pressure. Recognize that repayment schedules and credit scoring systems influence behavior across society, not only in your household.

When obligations are manageable relative to income, choices expand. When choices expand, risk can be evaluated thoughtfully rather than fearfully.

Ownership expands options. Options restore flexibility.

Returning to Adam, he wakes up at 6:15. He reviews his calendar. He knows what clears on the first, the fifteenth, and the twenty-second. For years, he has oriented his life around those dates. He is not trapped by visible force. He is anchored by payments.

If he understands the mechanism, he can begin adjusting it. He can reduce obligations gradually. He can build liquidity. He can acquire assets that produce income. He can design choices rather than react to schedules.

The system requires obligation. Debt becomes a tool that shapes behavior because it ties present conduct to future payment. When debt operates unconsciously, it narrows options quietly. When debt is understood, it can be directed intentionally.

To understand why the top tier of wealth expands steadily, you have to see how structured obligation below supports ownership above.

When you see the structure, you regain agency inside it.

That is where the shift begins.

CHAPTER 8

WHY THE TOP 1% KEEPS WINNING

Damian checks the market during lunch most afternoons, usually while standing in line or waiting for his coffee. The habit feels ordinary now, almost administrative, because financial markets have become part of the background noise of daily life. His phone shows the S&P 500 climbing from around 1,100 in 2010 to above 4,500 today, and the shape of that line carries its own message. Growth looks steady from a distance. Growth looks available.

The message becomes harder to trust once Damian returns to his own numbers. His rent has risen from $1,350 a month to $1,850 in five years. His grocery bill, which used to hover near $80 a week, now drifts closer to $120. His salary has increased during that same period, though the increase behaves differently from the cost of living. The paycheck arrives, and then it gets divided.

This gap between what people hear and what they feel has become one of the defining features of modern economic life. Financial news speaks in the language of expansion, records, and market gains. Many households speak in the language of tighter budgets, delayed purchases, and thinner margins. Both descriptions can be true at the same time. The key question is where the growth is landing.

That question sounds simple, though it opens into a whole discussion. When the economy grows, who owns the part that grows fastest? When markets rise, who is actually getting richer? Those questions matter because the modern economy creates wealth mainly through assets, and assets always belong to someone. Growth may look national. Ownership is always specific.

The clearest way to see that ownership is through the Survey of Consumer Finances, the Federal Reserve's detailed study of household balance sheets. The survey looks across the country and measures homes, retirement accounts, businesses, stocks, bonds, and debts. When researchers total those assets, U.S. household wealth recently stands above $150 trillion. That number is enormous, though its meaning depends entirely on how it is distributed.

The distribution is where the story changes. The top 1 percent of households owns about 31 percent of total U.S. wealth, which comes to more than $45 trillion. The bottom 50 percent owns about 2.6 percent, roughly $4 trillion spread across more than sixty million households. A society can describe itself as broad and middle-class, yet these numbers describe something steeper. Wealth exists. Its location is concentrated.

You can feel the shape of that concentration by shrinking the country into a room of one hundred households. One household in that room controls roughly one-third of everything. Fifty households divide a very small slice among themselves. The picture becomes even clearer when you imagine what wealth actually means in daily life: home equity, business ownership, investment accounts, land, and the capacity to wait when conditions turn difficult. The numbers are not simply large. They are directional.

At this point, the reader is entitled to ask a second question. What kind of wealth sits at the top of the pile?

Cash behaves one way. A business behaves another way. A house in a rising market behaves differently again. In the modern United States, some assets matter much more than others.

Stocks sit near the center of that answer because they are claims on corporate profits. When companies sell more, earn more, and expand, shareholders receive the gains through higher stock prices and dividend payments. Over long periods of time, that process has been remarkably powerful. From 1926 through 2025, U.S. stocks have returned about 10 percent a year before inflation, a figure that appears so often in investing literature because it changes everything once time enters the picture. Ten percent sounds modest until it compounds for decades.

The ownership of those stocks reveals an even sharper concentration than overall wealth. Federal Reserve data shows that the top 1 percent owns about 50 percent of all corporate equities and mutual funds. The bottom half of the population owns roughly 1 percent. Many families have some retirement exposure through a 401(k) or pension plan, and that matters. The larger truth remains intact. The bulk of stock-market ownership sits where wealth already sits.

That detail changes the meaning of a headline most readers have seen hundreds of times. When a news anchor says the stock market created $8 trillion in value in a strong year, the statement is numerically true. In 2021, U.S. equities gained more than that amount. Yet the gain did not spread across the country the way a weather system spreads rain. It appeared mainly on the balance sheets of households, funds, and institutions that already held large equity positions. A rising market is real wealth creation. It is also selective wealth creation.

You can see the same pattern in the way people talk about "the market" as if it were the economy itself. The market matters because it prices ownership claims on the country's most valuable companies. The economy matters because it includes wages, bills, rents, debt payments, and the lived reality of households. Those two things overlap, though they do not move in sync. When ownership is concentrated, the gains from the market are concentrated too.

This is the place where a basic distinction becomes useful.

- Income is what you earn through work.
- Wealth is what you own after subtracting what you owe.

Income pays for life as it is currently lived. Wealth changes what becomes possible over time. A household can earn a respectable salary and still build wealth slowly if housing, childcare, transportation, healthcare, and taxes absorb most of the paycheck. Another household can earn a moderate salary and still become much wealthier if it already owns assets that rise in value.

Once you separate income from wealth, the puzzle begins to clear. Income usually grows in increments. In many professions, wages rise by 3 to 5 percent a year during stable periods, with occasional jumps from promotions or job changes. Asset prices can move much faster.

Take a homeowner who bought a house for $300,000 before that surge. If the home is now worth $420,000, the household has gained $120,000 in wealth. That increase did not arrive as extra hours worked, extra meetings attended, or extra years of schooling completed during that period. It arrived because the asset appreciated. The house sat in the right market at the right time, and the owner's balance sheet rose with it.

Stocks work through the same logic, only with a different kind of asset. An investor who buys shares at $100 and watches them rise to $150 has gained 50 percent on that position. That increase may reflect stronger profits, better expectations, or wider enthusiasm in the market. The mechanism is less important here than the outcome. The value of the asset has increased, and the owner receives the gain.

You can feel the cumulative effect once you place those changes next to wage growth. Suppose one person earns $60,000 a year and grows that income to $80,000 over fifteen years. That is real progress and often hard-won progress. Suppose another person began the same period with $100,000 invested in a broad stock portfolio that roughly tracked the market's long rise from 2010 onward. That portfolio may now be worth more than $400,000, especially if dividends were reinvested. Both people moved forward. Their mechanisms of progress were very different.

That difference is the heart of the scoreboard. Wages help people live. Assets help people compound. Wages are usually tied to time, attention, and labor-market conditions. Assets are tied to ownership, market pricing, and scale. Once a society organizes wealth creation around assets, the distribution of assets begins to shape the distribution of opportunity itself. You have already seen the machinery behind this in earlier chapters. Credit expands. Financial conditions ease. Money reaches markets through particular channels. Asset prices often respond earlier than wages. Borrowing costs differ across the system. Those ideas explain why markets can rise so strongly. This chapter begins where those chapters left off. It asks what those repeated cycles produce after years and decades.

Households with significant assets receive the gains from rising asset prices, then they begin the next cycle with larger balance sheets. Larger balance sheets provide more investment capacity, more collateral, more room to hold through volatility, and more access to future gains. Households with few assets see less of that compounding, even when they work steadily and save carefully. Over time, the scoreboard becomes the fingerprint of that process.

Conversations about wealth often slide quickly into debates about character, as though the only available explanation were virtue on one side and failure on the other. Real life is more complicated and more structured. Effort matters. Skill matters. Discipline matters. Ownership matters too, and it matters in a way the culture often understates.

A rising stock market offers a good example of that understatement. News coverage treats the gain as a national event because the number itself is national. The experience of that gain is much narrower. The top 1 percent, which owns about half of all equities, experiences a market boom very differently from the bottom half, which owns about 1 percent. The same headline reaches both groups. The wealth effect lands in very different places.

That helps explain why Damian's phone and Damian's budget can seem to describe different countries. The chart on his screen is real. The squeeze in his monthly expenses is real too. The economy can create large amounts of wealth through assets while leaving many households with only a thin connection to that wealth. Once you see the ownership structure, the contradiction becomes easier to understand.

You can test that idea against your own memory of economic news. When commentators celebrate rising home prices, who already owns homes in appreciating markets? When the stock market posts record highs, who already holds large portfolios? When private business values climb, who already owns private businesses? Growth is often reported as a collective achievement.

So, if the rewards of growth go so heavily to the people who already own the assets, where does that leave everyone else? The answer begins in the next section, because the scoreboard shows only the result. To understand why the same households keep appearing near the top, we have to move from outcomes to starting positions, and from starting positions to leverage.

For now, the essential point is stability and clarity. The gap at the top is shaped by where the assets sit, because the gains from economic growth flow first to the people who already own them.

Position Matters More Than Effort

Two graduates can leave the same campus in the same month and enter very different financial lives, even when their effort looks remarkably similar. They studied hard, found decent jobs, and received starting salaries near $65,000 a year, which places them in a respectable early-career range for many American cities. Their résumés suggest discipline. Their futures seem open. From a distance, they appear to be starting the same race.

The difference enters quietly through the balance sheet. One graduate leaves school carrying $40,000 in student loans and signs a lease for $1,700 a month. The other graduate receives family help for a down payment on a $350,000 starter home, which turns a monthly housing payment into mortgage amortization and exposure to rising home values. The monthly outflow may look similar. The financial direction underneath it is very different.

This is one of the easiest places to miss how wealth actually forms. People tend to compare salaries because salaries are visible, socially legible, and easy to discuss. Wealth forms through what sits behind the salary. A paycheck keeps life moving. A balance sheet decides whether progress can compound.

If you follow the two graduates through the next decade, the divergence grows with surprising speed. Both work hard, collect promotions, and eventually earn somewhere between $95,000 and $110,000 a year. Their careers look healthy by ordinary standards. Yet the graduate who entered the housing market with family assistance is building equity each month while also benefiting from any appreciation in the home itself.

Suppose that home rises 35 percent over ten years, which would take a $350,000 property to roughly $472,000. Add a decade of mortgage payments, and the owner may hold $180,000 to $220,000 in home equity, depending on the loan structure and local market. The renter may have saved some money during that same period, and that matters. The owner, however, has been carried forward by an appreciating asset that the renter never controlled.

That difference often begins small enough to look harmless. A parent helps with a down payment. A relative funds a retirement account. A family member pays for graduate school. These gestures can feel like temporary assistance. Over time they behave more like launch advantages because assets compound, debts require servicing, and the gap between owning and paying widens in slow motion.

You can probably see versions of this in your own surroundings. Some people begin adult life with a cushion, a family network, a first investment account, or access to property. Others begin with rent, debt, and almost no room for error. The contrast does not always announce itself loudly. It reveals itself later, often after a decade has passed and one person's finances seem to have "taken off."

The data on inheritance helps explain why these starting differences persist across generations. Federal Reserve research based on the Survey of Consumer Finances shows that the largest inheritances flow toward households that are already near the top of the wealth distribution. In one widely cited analysis, the top 10 percent of households received more than half of all inheritances, while the bottom half received a much smaller share. Wealth, in other words, often remains in the neighborhoods where wealth already lives.

This matters because inheritance does more than transfer money. It transfers timing. A family gift received at age twenty-eight can become a down payment, seed capital, or a debt-free start during the years when compounding has the most room to work. The same dollar received at age sixty-five has a different effect. The transfer changes the path because it changes the starting line.

Once you see that, a deeper mechanism comes into view. Wealth grows fastest when ownership is paired with *leverage*.

Leverage sounds technical, though the idea is simple. It means controlling a large asset with a smaller amount of your own cash. A mortgage is the most familiar example. A household may purchase a $400,000 home with 20 percent down, which means contributing $80,000 and borrowing the remaining $320,000. The buyer controls the entire home while supplying only part of the capital.

That arrangement becomes powerful when prices rise. If the house appreciates by 10 percent, its value moves from $400,000 to $440,000. The increase equals $40,000, which amounts to a 50 percent gain on the original $80,000 down payment, even before considering mortgage amortization. The owner captured the movement of the whole asset. That is the force of leverage.

The same principle appears throughout modern finance. Investors borrow against portfolios to buy more securities. Private equity firms buy companies with a mixture of investor money and debt. Commercial real estate investors finance buildings with large loans and relatively small equity stakes. Institutions near the center of the financial system become skilled at this because leverage allows assets to do work at a scale labor rarely can.

You do not need a hedge fund to see the point. Look again at housing between 2012 and 2022, when U.S. home prices rose by more than 110 percent, according to the Federal Housing Finance Agency. A buyer who put $60,000 down on a $300,000 home and saw that property rise to $630,000 captured $330,000 in appreciation while starting with a fraction of that amount. The asset moved. The balance sheet absorbed the movement. The original cash contribution did not have to grow dollar by dollar through work.

This is where effort begins to encounter its limit. Labor income is earned in sequence. You work an hour, a day, a year, and receive compensation through time. A salary can rise meaningfully across a career, especially for skilled workers. A worker earning $70,000 who receives average raises of 3 percent a year will make steady progress. The pace remains tied to employment, negotiation, and the clock. Assets operate under a different math. A stock portfolio can rise while its owner is asleep. A house can appreciate while its owner is at work. A business can generate profits through the labor of employees, systems, and scale. That difference matters because it separates earning from owning. One is powerful. The other compounds.

You can feel the distinction in a simple phrase. Hard work produces income. Ownership paired with leverage produces wealth.

The structure grows even stronger once policy enters the picture. In the United States, long-term capital gains face a top federal rate of 20 percent, with an additional 3.8 percent surtax for some high earners, bringing the combined top rate to 23.8 percent. Wage income faces a top federal marginal rate of 37 percent, and payroll taxes still sit on top of much of labor income. The tax code therefore places different weights on different forms of gain. This difference developed through policy choices made over many decades. Lawmakers have often defended lower capital gains rates as a way to encourage investment and support growth. That debate has been going on for a long time, and it is likely to continue. The practical effect is easier to state than the political argument. Income from assets often keeps more of itself than income from labor.

Once you notice that, corporate behavior starts to look different as well. Public companies routinely direct large amounts of cash to shareholders through dividends and stock repurchases. In 2022, firms in the S&P 500 spent more than $900 billion on stock buybacks alone. Those buybacks tend to support earnings per share and, under many conditions, share prices as well. The people who benefit first are the people who already own the shares.

That sequence tells you something important about how success travels through the system. A company can have an excellent year, and the earliest financial reward may appear on the balance sheets of investors long before it appears in wage growth. Employees can benefit too, especially in strong firms and tight labor markets. The timing is still uneven. Ownership usually stands closer to the front of the line.

This is one reason the system often looks fairer than it behaves. Many societies hold tightly to the belief that effort and talent sit at the center of success. That belief is comforting because it maps neatly onto everyday experience. Children study and get better grades. Athletes train and improve. Workers who perform well often advance. The logic feels natural, so people carry it into questions of wealth.

The problem is not that merit plays no role. The problem is that merit can hide the machinery sitting around it. When starting positions differ, when assets appreciate, when leverage amplifies those gains, and when tax structures treat asset income more gently, the final outcome reflects much more than effort. The result still arrives wearing the familiar clothes of merit, which makes it harder to examine calmly.

That is why position matters so much. Position determines whether your monthly housing payment is building someone else's equity or your own. Position determines whether a rising market feels like distant good news or a direct increase in household wealth. Position determines whether borrowed money becomes a tool for buying assets or a burden attached to consumption. The same economy can produce very different outcomes because people enter it from different places.

Income usually arrives at the end of the process, after labor has been exchanged for pay. Ownership sits closer to the beginning because it receives the gains produced by assets, scale, and leverage. Those who begin near ownership often move forward earlier and faster. Those who begin near wages often advance through narrower channels. Over long stretches of time, this difference becomes visible in the national wealth numbers we saw in the first section. The scoreboard reflects more than work ethic. It reflects starting position, inherited advantage, leverage, policy, and the simple fact that assets compound more efficiently than paychecks. That is why wealth concentrates where ownership already has a foothold.

Offense and Defense

Two households can live on the same street, read the same headlines, and still inhabit very different economies. They hear the same reports about inflation, interest rates, and stock market swings. They shop at the same grocery stores and watch the same news anchors explain why the economy is changing. From the outside, their lives may even look equally careful and responsible. The difference appears when the economy applies pressure.

One household owns assets that can carry part of the financial load. They have a retirement account worth $750,000, a brokerage account holding roughly $300,000 in stocks and index funds, and a rental property originally purchased for $420,000. The second household relies mainly on wages. They earn about $85,000 a year, keep $6,000 in savings, and still owe $18,000 on a car loan. Both households budget. Only one balance sheet contains enough stored flexibility to change how bad news feels.

That difference becomes visible during a downturn. Imagine stock prices falling 20 percent over several months, the kind of drop the market experienced in 2000, 2008, and again during the early shock of 2020. Imagine rates rising, hiring slowing, and business owners becoming more cautious. None of this is unusual in a modern cycle. The economy tightens, and households find out what they are really standing on.

The asset-owning household sees its brokerage account fall from $300,000 to $240,000 on paper, which is unpleasant and real. Yet the rental property still throws off income, the retirement account remains invested, and the household has enough reserves to wait. Waiting matters because a temporary loss behaves very differently when you are free to leave it alone. Time changes the emotional meaning of volatility. Time turns a market drop into an event that can be survived without forced action.

The wage-dependent household experiences the same downturn through a different set of questions. What happens if overtime disappears for a few months? What happens if one paycheck arrives late, or one employer cuts hours, or one car repair lands at the wrong moment? A market correction may remain background noise to this family, though a slowdown in wages or hours lands immediately. The same downturn reaches both homes. It enters through different doors.

This is where a simple phrase becomes useful. Assets buy time. Time does more than reduce stress. Time changes the available choices. A household with savings, investments, and income-producing assets can delay decisions, absorb volatility, and avoid selling at moments of weakness. A household living closer to the edge has fewer options because ordinary disruptions arrive with greater force. Financial flexibility is not only a comfort. It is a strategic advantage.

The Federal Reserve's own household surveys make this easier to see. In recent years, about 37 percent of adults reported difficulty covering a $400 emergency expense using cash or its equivalent. That number is startling because $400 is not a major financial event in the grand language of economics. It is a car repair, a dental visit, a plane ticket for a family emergency, or a utility bill that arrived during the wrong month. For millions of households, small shocks still require borrowing, delay, or sacrifice.

Once you understand that, you start to see two different financial modes operating inside the same country. Some households spend most of their energy protecting stability. Others can use instability to their advantage. These are not personality types. They are positions inside a structure.

The first mode is defense. A household in defense protects the paycheck, avoids major risk, delays optional spending, and tries to keep the monthly machinery of life running smoothly. This approach makes perfect sense when a missed payment can trigger fees, stress, credit damage, or deeper debt. Defense is rational because fragility is expensive. A person standing on narrow footing learns caution very quickly.

The second mode is offense. A household in offense thinks about buying assets, adding to investments, refinancing intelligently, and using downturns to improve long-term position. That posture also makes sense because volatility looks different when the rent is covered, the emergency fund is full, and the portfolio does not need to be sold next month. Offense does not require optimism. It requires room.

You can probably recognize these two modes from your own life or from people around you. When money feels tight, the future shrinks toward the next bill, the next payment, the next week. When money feels secure, the future stretches. A market decline starts to resemble a lower entry price. A recession begins to look like a period that will eventually pass. The facts are the same. The interpretation changes with the balance sheet.

This is one reason wealth compounds so effectively across time. Investors who own substantial assets can remain in the market through bad years because they are not being asked to turn temporary losses into permanent ones. The S&P 500 has suffered multiple declines of 20 percent or more since 1980, including the crashes of 2000, 2008, and 2020. Over that same stretch, the index rose from roughly 135 to more than 4,500, a gain of more than 3,200 percent before counting dividends. Staying invested through that journey mattered more than predicting every twist along the way.

The ability to stay invested, however, is unevenly distributed. A household with deep reserves can keep buying through a downturn, reinvest dividends, and let time do the work. A household under pressure may stop retirement contributions, draw down savings, or liquidate assets at the very moment when long-term returns are becoming more attractive. The market eventually recovers. Some households were able to wait inside that recovery. Others had to step out before it arrived.

That difference produces a pattern that looks mysterious until you view it over several cycles. Expansions raise asset prices and increase the wealth of those who already own them. Recessions push prices lower and create opportunities for households with cash, credit access, and emotional room to act. The same families who benefit most during the rise often have the capacity to buy during the fall. Wealth therefore grows in good times and strengthens its position during bad times.

You might ask whether this is simply a matter of discipline. Discipline matters, though it behaves differently under different conditions. A household with $1 million in diversified assets can afford patience because daily life does not depend on liquidating those assets. A household with $6,000 in savings and no margin for unemployment practices a different kind of discipline. Their discipline appears as caution, restraint, and a refusal to gamble with essential stability. The system rewards the first form more generously because it is attached to ownership.

Researchers who study scarcity have found that limited resources can narrow attention and consume mental bandwidth. That effect shows up in everyday money management. A household preoccupied with rent, food, fuel, insurance, and debt service is operating under constant short-term demands. Long-range planning becomes harder because urgent needs are always arriving first. The issue here is not intelligence. The issue is pressure.

The broader financial system tends to amplify this divide. During strong years, asset prices can rise 15 to 20 percent, home values can climb sharply, and investors can borrow against growing collateral to purchase still more assets. During weak years, policymakers often move quickly to stabilize credit markets, support liquidity, and restore confidence in financial assets. Those responses matter because households with portfolios are positioned to benefit once markets rebound. The recovery reaches their balance sheets early.

Wage earners experience the same cycle with a delay. Recessions can bring layoffs, reduced hours, weaker bargaining power, and slower wage growth. The labor market may heal gradually even after asset markets have already snapped back. A stock portfolio can recover in months. Household income often takes longer. The sequence repeats often enough that it begins to define the modern economy.

This helps explain why the phrase "the rich get richer" can sound moralistic when the underlying mechanism is highly structural. Wealth changes how households experience time, risk, and downturns. It changes who can wait, who can buy, who can borrow, and who can recover quickly. The advantage is cumulative because each cycle leaves the stronger balance sheet with more strength than before. Once that process runs for decades, the result starts to look inevitable.

The offense-and-defense distinction is useful because it turns a vague feeling into a visible structure. A family in defense is trying to preserve its position. A family in offense is trying to improve its position by using time, assets, and volatility more effectively. Both are responding logically to the circumstances they face. The outcomes differ because the circumstances differ.

Damian's lunchtime puzzle should feel clearer at this point. The market can rise while many households feel pressure because the benefits of rising asset prices flow first to those who already own assets. The same logic applies during downturns. The households with room to act gain options, while the households under pressure focus on preserving stability. Over time, the difference between offense and defense becomes one of the quiet engines of wealth concentration.

This is why the top of the system keeps extending its lead. Ownership produces gains during expansions. Flexibility preserves those gains during downturns. Liquidity turns weak markets into opportunities. The pattern becomes easier to see once you stop treating all households as if they are playing the same game with the same tools. They are living under the same economy, though they are responding from very different positions within it.

The larger point is steady enough to carry forward. Wealth does more than increase comfort, because it changes the time horizon and the available choices, and those changes shape who can play offense while everyone else is still protecting the ground beneath them.

CHAPTER 9

BEATING INFLATION IS NOT OPTIONAL

Finn noticed the problem in a place where financial ideas rarely announce themselves. He was standing in a grocery line on a weekday evening, holding the same kind of basket he usually bought each week: milk, vegetables, chicken, bread, a few household basics. The total came up higher than he expected, and he paused for a second before paying. The basket looked familiar. The number did not.

Finn earns about $100,000 a year as a project manager outside Dallas. His income arrives on schedule every two weeks, his raises usually land in the two-to-four-percent range, and he saves regularly. He contributes to retirement, keeps a cash cushion, and avoids the kind of financial drama that usually signals trouble. From the outside, he looks like someone who is doing what responsible adults are supposed to do.

That is what made the feeling so strange. His life was stable, his income was steady, and his habits had improved over time. Yet the cost of ordinary life kept drifting upward in ways he could feel more easily than explain. Rent renewals came back a little higher, insurance premiums rose with each cycle, and dinner with friends cost just enough more to register in the back of his mind.

Eventually he opened a spreadsheet and did the kind of comparison most people postpone until something starts to feel off. He looked at grocery bills, utilities, rent, and other monthly expenses from a few years earlier. The pattern was not dramatic in any single category. It was simply consistent, and consistency is what gives a financial pattern its force.

At first he suspected the usual culprit: himself. People often interpret financial pressure as a sign of personal slippage, so they search for waste, weak discipline, or small indulgences that somehow multiplied. Finn did the same thing. He reviewed statements, checked receipts, and found that his routines were basically unchanged.

That is when the real puzzle came into view. His paycheck had grown modestly over time, and his savings balance had grown with it. Yet the life those numbers could buy felt slightly smaller than before. The squeeze was real, though it had arrived without a clear event to blame.

Economists call it inflation, which simply means that prices across the economy rise over time. The definition sounds tidy. The lived experience feels much less tidy because inflation rarely arrives as a single shock. It moves through thousands of small price adjustments until the overall pattern becomes visible.

That gradual quality is what makes inflation so easy to underestimate. A gallon of milk that costs $3.50 this year may cost $3.60 next year, and the difference feels too small to command attention. When the same quiet movement happens across food, rent, healthcare, transportation, and education, the monthly budget changes even when no single receipt looks alarming. Inflation operates through accumulation, which is why it often becomes obvious only in retrospect.

The arithmetic becomes clearer when you stretch the timeline. Imagine prices rising by a cumulative 24 percent over a certain period. A salary that once bought $100,000 worth of life now buys something closer to $76,000 worth of that same life. The paycheck still says $100,000. The purchasing power behind that number has shifted.

We tend to think in nominal terms because nominal terms are the ones printed on paychecks, bank statements, and financial apps. They are visible, precise, and emotionally reassuring. Purchasing power is harder to see because it lives outside the account, in the changing prices of the world around you.

The United States has lived with this pattern for a long time. Over more than a century, inflation has averaged roughly 3 percent annually, though it has moved higher and lower across different decades. Three percent sounds small, and in a single year it usually feels small. Across ten or twenty years, it changes the meaning of almost every financial number a household relies on. A simple example shows why. If prices rise by 3 percent a year, something that costs $100 today costs about $134 in ten years and around $180 in twenty years. Nothing spectacular has to happen for that change to matter. Time does the work quietly, which is why inflation feels less like a crisis and more like a slow revision of everyday life.

For a long time, households could partly offset this pressure through ordinary saving. During some periods in the twentieth century, savings accounts paid interest rates that roughly matched inflation or even exceeded it. In parts of the 1970s and 1980s, for instance, bank savings rates could rise above 5 percent. In that environment, the old advice to save cash and stay patient made practical sense because the bank account did some of the defensive work for you.

That world changed. In the early 2010s, many U.S. savings accounts paid well under 1 percent while inflation often ran around 2 to 3 percent. Put those numbers side by side and the problem becomes easy to see. If prices rise 3 percent and your savings earn 1 percent, your cash loses about 2 percent of its purchasing power over that year even while the balance inches upward. This is one of the quietest financial losses in modern life. The number in the account rises slightly, which creates the impression of progress. The value attached to that number slips slightly, which creates the reality of drift. Both things can happen at the same time.

A bank balance feels stable because it does not bounce around from day to day. You open the app, see a familiar figure, and receive a small sense of order. That emotional response is understandable. Stability on a screen feels like stability in life. Markets feel different. Stocks rise and fall every day, sometimes for reasons that seem obscure or arbitrary, and that movement creates discomfort. Many people would rather hold an asset with a quiet number than one with a noisy price, even when the noisy asset has a much better long-term record of preserving purchasing power. The preference makes emotional sense. Financially, it often comes at a cost.

This is why inflation can hide inside responsible behavior. A diligent saver may build a larger cash balance year after year and still fall behind in real terms. The account shows discipline. The economy applies its own arithmetic. Those two realities can sit side by side for years before the gap becomes obvious.

One of the clearest ways to see that gap is to compare cash with productive assets over a long stretch of time. Over the past century, the U.S. stock market has returned roughly 9 to 10 percent annually on average, including dividends. Inflation over that same period has averaged around 3 percent. The difference between those numbers may look modest in a single year. Over decades it becomes enormous.

Take a simple historical example. If you had invested $10,000 in a broad U.S. stock index in 1970 and reinvested dividends, that investment would be worth well over $2 million today, depending on the index used. Hold the same $10,000 as cash, and the nominal balance remains $10,000 while the purchasing power falls sharply. One path participates in the growth of the economy. The other waits while the measuring stick changes.

Once you see this, Finn's problem stops looking personal. His salary was rising. His savings habit was solid. His financial pressure came from a system in which money can hold its face value while losing part of its real value year after year. He was reading his life in nominal terms while living it in real terms. You may be doing some version of the same thing. The number in your savings account is a real number, and it matters. The purchasing power of that number matters more because purchasing power determines what your savings can actually do for you later. A stable balance can still mask a shrinking claim on the future.

This is the first important shift. Inflation is not a special event reserved for bad years or economic headlines. It is a continuing feature of modern life, shaped by broad forces such as monetary policy, government spending, supply chains, and long-term economic growth. You may not control those forces, though you live inside their consequences every day. That is why the real question is where your savings spend their time while inflation keeps moving. They can sit in forms that preserve the visible number, or they can move into assets that have historically grown with the economy and often faster than inflation. Over a few months, the difference feels small. Over a few decades, it defines the outcome.

Finn's grocery bill was a small signal from a much larger system, and once he recognized it, the rest of his financial life began to look different. Inflation keeps changing what money can buy, which means any serious plan has to begin with purchasing power.

Why Assets Rise While Money Sleeps

Imagine a household that took on a $900 monthly mortgage in 1995. At the time, $900 represented a serious commitment. Over the following decades, incomes rose across the economy, groceries cost more, services cost more, and rent climbed in many cities. The mortgage payment still read $900, though the purchasing power of that $900 had changed substantially. Inflation had quietly reduced the real burden of the debt.

That is one of the hidden advantages of long-term fixed borrowing tied to a real asset. The homeowner owns something that may rise in price while repaying the loan with future dollars that are worth less than the dollars originally borrowed. The asset and the debt move through the same economy, though they respond to it in very different ways. Over time, that difference can become one of the most powerful wealth-building mechanics in ordinary middle-class life.

The renter experiences the same inflation from the opposite side of the table. Rent adjusts as property values rise, taxes rise, maintenance costs rise, and landlords reprice the use of the asset. The renter therefore meets inflation as a recurring expense. The homeowner often meets that same inflation as rising equity and a mortgage payment that becomes easier to carry in real terms.

Inflation does not land evenly. Two households can live under the same monetary system and experience opposite financial outcomes because one owns an asset while the other pays to access it. The same economy produces rising pressure for one and rising leverage for the other. Once you notice that pattern in housing, you begin to see it elsewhere. Inflation changes the value of currency over time, though assets connected to real economic life often adjust upward with it. Cash sits still in nominal terms. Assets tend to move because they are claims on land, production, energy, businesses, or scarcity itself.

That last word matters more than it first appears to. Scarcity tends to hold its value when currency becomes more abundant. Dollars can expand through lending, deficit spending, and broader financial growth. Land in a good location expands slowly. A productive business expands through effort and demand, which is a different process entirely. Gold expands slowly because mining is difficult, expensive, and time-consuming.

The 1970s offer a useful illustration of this instinct. During that decade, inflation surged, trust in paper money weakened, and investors began looking for assets that could preserve purchasing power. Gold, which had traded near $35 an ounce in 1971, rose above $800 by 1980. That move looked dramatic on a price chart, though underneath it sat a very old human response: when money feels easier to create, people start searching for things that are harder to create. Gold mattered during that period because its supply grew slowly. New deposits have to be discovered, extracted, refined, and brought to market through a long industrial process. Annual supply growth remains modest compared with the existing stock. In an inflationary environment, that slow supply growth becomes financially meaningful because scarcity begins to look like protection.

You can see a similar instinct in the modern fascination with Bitcoin. People argue endlessly about its long-term role, its volatility, and its place in a serious portfolio. Yet the emotional logic behind its appeal is easy to understand. Bitcoin's supply is capped at 21 million coins, and that fixed limit gives investors something fiat currency does not provide: a rule against endless expansion.

The deeper pattern here is older than either gold or Bitcoin. Whenever people suspect that money will buy less in the future, they begin asking what can hold value better than money itself. In one generation the answer might be land. In another, it might be gold, stocks, real estate, or a new kind of digital asset built around scarcity. The forms change. The instinct remains remarkably consistent.

So where does that leave you?

It leaves you with a question that becomes hard to ignore once you have seen the pattern clearly. If currency can expand over time, and if that expansion gradually weakens purchasing power, where should your savings live? Inside cash alone, the answer is limited. Inside assets tied to the real economy, the answer begins to widen.

This does not mean every asset rises smoothly or safely. Housing markets cool, stocks fall, commodities swing, and speculative manias appear whenever a good idea attracts too much excitement. Yet over long stretches of time, assets tied to production, scarcity, and real economic demand have behaved very differently from idle cash. That difference is the point.

From Victim to Strategist

At this point, you have already seen the pattern: money expands, prices adjust, and assets usually respond differently than idle cash. The question is no longer what inflation is doing. The question becomes what you are going to do in response.

A useful place to begin is with the people who think about this problem for a living. Pension funds, insurance companies, and university endowments manage money for obligations that stretch decades into the future. A pension fund may need to pay retirees thirty years from now. An endowment may need to support scholarships long after the current trustees are gone. That kind of responsibility forces a very different way of thinking.

Institutions like these do not judge success by asking whether the account balance is higher this year than last year. They ask whether the portfolio will preserve purchasing power across time. That sounds like a small difference in language. In practice, it changes everything. Once the target becomes future purchasing power, cash starts looking like a temporary holding place rather than a long-term plan.

That is why large pools of capital usually spread themselves across assets tied to the real economy. Pension funds own stocks because stocks are claims on productive businesses. They own real estate because it produces income and participates in long-term property markets. They often hold infrastructure and commodities for similar reasons: these assets connect to energy, transportation, land, and physical demand that continue to matter regardless of the financial mood of a given year.

You can see the logic without needing the scale of an institution. A retirement system that must meet obligations in 2045 or 2055 cannot rely on cash earning less than inflation for long stretches of time. Mathematics simply works against it. Institutions understand this at a structural level, which is why they build portfolios around real returns rather than nominal comfort.

That mindset matters because households often approach the same problem in a very different way. Most people are taught to think first about income, then about saving, and only later about where those savings should live. The sequence feels sensible because savings represent discipline, and discipline feels like progress. Yet in an inflationary system, the location of savings matters almost as much as the act of saving itself.

This is where strategy begins. Strategy starts when you stop asking whether your money is safe in nominal terms and start asking whether it is alive in real terms. Those are different questions. A stable balance can still lose ground, and a fluctuating asset can still build long-term purchasing power.

Once you see that distinction, another point follows naturally. Successful long-term investing usually depends less on prediction than on consistency. People often imagine that investing rewards the person with the best forecast, the sharpest timing, or the strongest opinions about where markets will go next. The evidence points somewhere calmer.

Over long stretches of time, investors who contribute regularly tend to do better than investors who wait for the perfect moment. That happens for a simple reason. Markets rise and fall in ways that stir emotion, and emotion is expensive. People usually feel safest after prices have risen and most fearful after prices have fallen, which means instinct often pushes them toward buying high and hesitating low.

Automation helps because it sidesteps that cycle. When money moves into investments on a schedule tied to a paycheck or monthly transfer, the strategy no longer depends on mood, headlines, or confidence. The contribution happens whether the market is cheerful or anxious. Over time, this transforms investing from a recurring judgment call into a durable habit.

That habit matters more than many people realize. Behavioral finance has shown for years that financial decisions deteriorate when fear and excitement take turns driving the process. During market declines, fear encourages delay. During market rallies, confidence encourages overreach. Automation reduces both temptations by placing the decision upstream, before the emotion arrives.

This is the practical side of becoming a strategist. It has less to do with brilliance than with structure. You set rules when you are calm, and those rules continue working when markets become noisy. A system like that does something very important for ordinary investors: it protects them from the version of themselves that responds too quickly to recent events.

Think about your own financial life in these terms. Your income arrives from work, business activity, or some combination of both. After expenses are paid, what remains becomes stored effort. The central decision is where that effort will wait for you. It can sit in cash and hold its face value, or it can live partly in assets that have historically grown with the economy and often faster than inflation.

This choice rarely feels urgent in a single month. A few hundred dollars moved into investments may seem too small to matter, especially when bills are immediate and the future feels abstract. Yet compounding gives weight to small decisions when they are repeated patiently. The first contribution matters less because of its size than because it establishes direction.

Direction is what separates a passive participant from a strategist. A passive participant earns, saves, and hopes the system will be kind. A strategist understands that the system has its own rules and chooses where to stand within them. That shift is quiet, though it changes the meaning of every financial decision that follows.

It also brings the chapter back to its core principle. Inflation continues with or without your attention. It moves through the economy through policy, credit, spending, supply conditions, and long-term growth that no single household controls. Your power begins at a different point. It begins with deciding how your savings respond to that environment.

If savings grow more slowly than inflation, purchasing power declines even while the account balance looks respectable. If savings participate in assets that grow with the economy, the picture changes over time. That is the practical dividing line. The goal is to place your stored effort where time works for you rather than against you.

You do not need a dramatic reinvention of your life. You need a clearer frame, a steadier process, and a willingness to think the way long-horizon capital already thinks. Once you do that, inflation stops being a mystery and starts becoming a condition you plan around.

The next chapter builds that plan into a framework. We will move from the insight that inflation must be outpaced to a more organized way of doing it: generating cash flow, acquiring assets that appreciate, protecting gains, and using leverage with discipline. The important shift begins here, with the decision to treat purchasing power as the real measure of progress.

That decision is what turns financial awareness into financial strategy.

CHAPTER 10

CAPL + DR (YOUR FRAMEWORK)

Late one evening, Spencer sat at his kitchen table with four balances open on his screen. His checking account held a few thousand dollars. His savings account showed almost $9,000. His retirement plan at work had climbed to about $46,000. A small brokerage account held a few technology stocks he had bought after reading about long-term investing. By any ordinary standard, Spencer looked responsible. He worked steadily, paid his bills, and paid attention.

The unease came from the way the pieces fit together. One credit card still carried a balance from a vacation taken the year before, and the rate on that balance was above 20 percent. His savings account earned less than 4 percent. When rent rose, he paused his monthly investment contributions for a while, then restarted them at a lower amount. Each choice had felt sensible at the time. Together, they produced a strange result. Spencer was making decisions, yet the decisions were not clearly building toward anything.

That pattern shows up in more households than we like to admit. Financial life is full of separate compartments: one account for spending, one for emergencies, one for retirement, one for debt, maybe one for investing. Each account has a purpose. Each decision has a reason. The trouble begins when those pieces live beside one another without a clear order or relationship. A household can look organized on the surface and still feel unsettled underneath.

You may recognize that feeling yourself. You save something, invest a little, pay down debt when you can, and try to stay informed. Then life shifts. A repair bill arrives. Insurance jumps. A job feels less secure. Suddenly the structure starts wobbling. Contributions stop. Credit balances rise. Plans that seemed sensible a month earlier become hard to maintain. The question is worth asking plainly: why does this happen so often to people who are trying to be careful?

The answer begins with a simple observation. Most people manage money one decision at a time. They do not usually build it as a sequence. A savings account opens when security feels important. A retirement account begins when an employer offers a match. A brokerage account appears after curiosity turns into action. A credit card becomes part of normal life because it solves a short-term problem efficiently. None of these decisions is unusual. The deeper issue is that they rarely arrive in an intentional order.

Richard Thaler, the behavioral economist, gave us a useful way to see this. He called it **mental accounting**. People divide money into separate mental buckets, then make decisions inside each bucket as if the rest of the household balance sheet were happening somewhere else. A tax refund feels different from a paycheck. Savings can feel untouchable even while credit card interest compounds nearby. An investment account can feel like the place where your future lives, while everyday financial stress keeps unfolding in another corner of the same household.

Once you see that pattern, ordinary behavior starts to look different. Someone can keep $10,000 in savings because it feels prudent and still carry a credit card balance at a double-digit rate. Those decisions sound responsible when considered one by one. Together they create drag. One pocket of money is earning a little, while another pocket is losing a lot more. The household is moving in two directions at once.

This is what makes personal finance more subtle than it first appears. The problem is often less about intelligence than about arrangement. People are not usually confused by arithmetic. They are navigating money through categories that feel emotionally real: safety, progress, obligation, freedom. Those categories make everyday life manageable, yet they can also hide the larger structure. A person can feel disciplined and still be caught in a design that works against itself.

Spencer's situation becomes clearer when you look at it this way. He had not made reckless choices. He had made familiar choices. He saved because saving felt wise. He invested because he knew he should think long term. He carried some debt because life had costs and timing mattered. The weakness in the system came from order. His decisions were sitting next to one another rather than supporting one another.

The economy has a way of exposing that hidden weakness. The Federal Reserve's Survey of Household Economics and Decisionmaking asks Americans how they would handle an unexpected **$400** expense. In recent years, roughly one-third have said they would need to borrow, sell something, or miss a payment. That number carries more weight than it first seems to. It tells us many households are living with very little space between incoming money and outgoing obligation.

That narrow space changes behavior. A car repair, medical bill, or interrupted paycheck does more than create an expense. It changes the time horizon of the whole household. Long-term decisions get postponed because short-term pressures move to the front of the line. Investing pauses. Debt becomes a bridge. Plans turn into reactions. A household may still look functional from the outside, though internally it has shifted into a more fragile mode.

This is one reason public conversations about money often miss the point. They assume the main problem is a shortage of discipline or information. Save more. Spend less. Invest early. Avoid bad debt. Build an emergency fund. Most of that advice is sound, and almost all of it is incomplete. Advice given without order turns into noise. A household can follow several good rules at once and still feel financially scattered because the rules are not arranged into a system.

That narrowing effect changes what money feels like. Instead of acting as a tool for shaping the future, it starts behaving like a sequence of interruptions. You deal with one issue, then another. You move money from one account, pause something else, carry a balance for a while, promise yourself you will straighten it out next month. Each move is understandable. The pattern, over time, becomes exhausting. The household is active, though it is not advancing in a clear direction.

Once you notice this, another realization begins to emerge. Many people do not need more financial tips. They need a structure that tells them what belongs first, what belongs later, and what only works once the earlier stages are in place. Without that order, it is easy to reach for advanced strategies before the base can support them. Someone invests aggressively without much margin. Someone else hoards cash while purchasing power quietly erodes. Another person focuses on eliminating every debt while missing chances to build productive assets. The choices can all sound rational. The sequence is where the real difference appears.

That is where CAPL + DR enters the picture. The framework organizes financial behavior into a cycle: **Cashflow, Appreciation, Protection, Leverage, and De-Risking**. The letters matter less than the order. Each stage prepares the next stage. Each stage also changes what kind of decision makes sense after it. When you see money this way, the chaos begins to sort itself into a pattern.

That shift in perspective can be surprisingly practical. Instead of asking, "Should I invest now?" or "Should I pay off this debt first?" you begin by asking a better question: where am I in the cycle? The question sounds simple, though it changes how decisions relate to one another. A savings account stops being just a savings account. Debt stops being just debt. Investing stops being a separate activity done when confidence happens to be high. Each piece gets assigned a role.

When Spencer looked at his finances through that lens, his accounts did not suddenly become wrong or right. They became easier to understand. The issue was no longer whether he was a saver, an investor, or a borrower. The issue was whether his choices were arranged in an order that let one part strengthen the next. Once that became clear, his financial life looked less like a collection of habits and more like a structure waiting to be organized.

CAPL + DR - The Sequence

Once you understand why so many households feel financially busy and financially unclear at the same time, the next question becomes easier to ask. What would a real system look like? What kind of order would turn scattered effort into forward movement?

CAPL + DR answers that question by giving each financial stage a role, a sequence, and a reason.

The power of the framework sits in the order. Many people already do some version of these things. They earn, save, invest, borrow, and adjust. The trouble usually begins when those actions happen in the wrong sequence, or when one stage is asked to do the work of another. A system helps because it tells you what belongs first, what belongs next, and what only works well after the earlier layers are in place.

You can think of CAPL + DR as five linked stages:

1. Cashflow
2. Appreciation
3. Protection
4. Leverage
5. De-Risking

Each stage solves a different problem. Each stage also prepares the next one. That is why the framework works as a sequence rather than a list.

Cashflow - the base layer

Cashflow comes first because pressure always comes first. A household that lives too close to its monthly obligations will struggle to hold any long-term plan together, no matter how good that plan looks on paper. A rent increase, a car repair, a medical bill, or a stretch of reduced income can force immediate decisions. Under those conditions, the future keeps getting interrupted by the present.

That is why cashflow matters more than it first seems. Cashflow creates margin. It creates time. It gives the household a little room between what life costs and what the system produces. That room changes behavior because it reduces the need to solve every surprise with debt, liquidation, or panic. You begin to think less like a person putting out fires and more like a person building something durable.

Cashflow as more than wages. The goal is to build streams of income that can grow faster than the cost of living. That might include rental income, dividend-paying assets, small business income, royalties, or other recurring sources tied to ownership. A system cannot grow calmly until it can breathe.

In the next chapter, we will slow down and look at cashflow on its own. We will examine how it is built, why it changes your decision-making, and why it becomes the fuel for everything that follows. For now, it is enough to see why it belongs at the beginning. Cashflow gives the rest of the structure a chance to hold.

Appreciation - turning stability into growth

Once cashflow begins creating consistent surplus, a new question appears. What should that surplus do? If it simply sits still forever, inflation keeps working quietly in the background. The dollars remain visible, though their purchasing power keeps changing. Stability, on its own, helps you endure. Over time, you also need growth.

That is where appreciation enters the sequence. Appreciation means directing surplus cashflow into assets that tend to grow in value across long stretches of time. Real estate, stocks, and certain cryptocurrencies, especially where scarcity and long-term demand are present. The Stability must eventually be converted into ownership that can outpace inflation.

This is the point where many people try to begin, which helps explain why so many plans feel shaky. Growth is attractive. Growth is visible. Growth feels like progress. Yet growth is much harder to sustain when the system underneath it remains fragile. An investor with weak cashflow often understands what to do, then finds it difficult to stay with the plan when life becomes expensive. In practice, appreciation works best when cashflow has already lowered the emotional temperature of the household.

First you create enough breathing room to stop every short-term problem from taking over the whole system. Then you direct some of that room into assets that can grow. The next chapter after cashflow will take appreciation apart in detail, because appreciation has its own rules, its own risks, and its own forms of patience. Here, we only need the architectural truth: cashflow stabilizes, and appreciation expands.

Protection - keeping growth from turning into fragility

Growth introduces a new problem, and it is one many people fail to notice until a cycle turns against them. At the beginning, the main challenge is building. Later, the main challenge becomes keeping what has been built. A rising asset changes your position, though it also changes your exposure. Gains create confidence, and confidence can quietly create concentration, complacency, or unnecessary risk.

Protection belongs in the framework because every cycle eventually changes character. Markets heat up. Valuations stretch. Assets that once looked attractively priced begin to look expensive. During those periods, protection means shifting some gains into more stable positions, lower-risk holdings, or cash reserves. The purpose is to preserve optionality and reduce the chance that one reversal undoes too much progress.

This idea often looks dull in prosperous periods. Protective capital can seem passive when everything around it is rising. Then conditions shift, and the value of protection becomes much clearer. Liquidity during a boom can look underused. Liquidity during a panic becomes power. The distinction matters because the same reserve that appears quiet in one season often becomes strategic in the next.

We will examine protection carefully in its own chapter, including what it means to defend gains without stepping out of the game entirely. Here, the basic role is enough. Protection changes the question from "How do I grow?" to "How do I stay strong when the cycle changes?" That is a different problem, which is why it deserves its own stage.

Leverage - a later-stage tool

Leverage comes later for a reason. People are naturally drawn to it because leverage looks powerful, and sometimes it is. Borrowed money can increase purchasing power, amplify returns, and allow a person to act more aggressively when opportunities appear. The danger is that leverage does not ask whether the system beneath it is stable. It simply magnifies whatever is already there.

That is why leverage belongs after cashflow, appreciation, and protection. When the cycle turns and asset prices come down, leverage can be used to buy into weakness at more favorable prices. In the client brief, this is the moment when appreciating assets are cheaper again, and borrowed capital can help repeat the cycle. Used from a position of stability, leverage becomes an accelerator. Used from a position of fragility, it becomes stress with interest attached.

A household without margin can be damaged by leverage very quickly. A household with stable cashflow, growing assets, and protective reserves stands in a very different place. The tool is the same. The outcome changes because the sequence changes. That is the deeper lesson.

De-Risking - the ongoing discipline

De-risking sits at the end of the acronym, though it really runs through the entire cycle. It is the habit that keeps the system awake. Conditions change. Markets move. Inflation shifts. Concentration grows quietly. Confidence can rise faster than judgment. A framework without adjustment eventually becomes stale because real life keeps moving.

That is why de-risking is continuous rather than occasional. It means asking simple questions at regular intervals. Has one asset grown too large? Has a strong run created hidden exposure? Are current positions still suitable for the current stage of the cycle? Those questions are not dramatic, though they are essential. They keep the system from drifting too far in one direction.

De-risking also protects you from a common human mistake. People often assume that motion is the same as control. In practice, constant motion usually reflects emotional management rather than strategic management. A disciplined system does not react to every headline or every market swing. It adjusts with purpose. It reduces exposure where exposure has grown too large. It preserves gains where gains have become vulnerable. It remains ready for the next move because it has not become overcommitted to the last one.

The reason CAPL + DR works is simple enough to say and hard enough to live. Each stage prepares the next one.

- **Cashflow** creates room.
- **Appreciation** turns room into growth.
- **Protection** preserves flexibility.
- **Leverage** expands opportunity when the structure can support it.
- **De-risking** keeps the whole system aligned as conditions change.

That order gives each financial decision a context. You stop asking isolated questions and start asking sequence-based questions. You stop treating every account and every tactic as a separate little world. You begin to see the whole household as one moving structure.

You are not meant to master all five parts here. This chapter is only introducing the map. The chapters ahead will slow the process down and examine each stage one by one, with examples, tactics, and practical decisions. We begin next with cashflow because cashflow changes the emotional and structural base of financial life. Once that foundation is clear, the rest of the system becomes easier to understand and far easier to sustain.

That is what this framework offers at the beginning: not certainty, and not perfection, but an order you can trust.

FREE GIFT: Watch The full CAPL+DR System Training

You just covered a powerful concept. And here's the truth information alone doesn't change your life. Execution does. So I created something for you. I put together a step-by-step video training where I walk you through exactly how to apply everything youjust learned, and take it even further. You can watch it for free. No opt in. No catch. Just scan the QR code or go to https://3twarrioracademy.com/training-capldr

SCAN ME

CHAPTER 11

CASH FLOW

March 16, 2020 offered a useful financial lesson because it compressed fear into a single trading day. As the pandemic spread, travel slowed, offices emptied, and markets began reacting to a world that suddenly looked fragile. By the closing bell, the S&P 500 had fallen nearly 12 percent, one of its sharpest daily drops since 2008. Millions of people spent that afternoon doing the same thing: opening an app and looking at a smaller future.

The losses felt especially sharp because the numbers had looked so calm only weeks earlier. Retirement accounts, college savings plans, and taxable portfolios had become part of ordinary life for the American middle class. People checked them between meetings, after dinner, or while waiting in line for coffee. Then one day the screen turned red, and the same account that had represented progress began to look like exposure.

That moment revealed a quiet divide between two kinds of investors.

One investor relied almost entirely on wages, and his portfolio served two jobs at once. It represented future wealth, and it also sat in the background as emergency protection if work became uncertain. When the market fell, his account stopped feeling like an investment and started feeling like a shrinking reserve. A second investor looked at the same falling market and felt the same concern, though her account told a slightly different story. Alongside the decline in market value, a dividend payment landed from one company she owned. A few days later another payment arrived from another holding. The amounts were ordinary, though the message was powerful. Her assets were still sending money back to her while prices were falling. Both investors owned investments. Both faced the same headlines and the same uncertainty. One saw only lower prices. The other saw lower prices and continuing income, which meant she had more room to wait.

This is where cashflow enters the conversation. Cashflow is money that arrives because something you own keeps working. A paycheck depends on your hours, your role, and your employer's willingness to keep paying you. Cashflow depends on an asset participating in the economy and sending part of that activity back to you as income.

The distinction sounds technical until pressure arrives. Under calm conditions, wage income and ownership income can look similar because both appear as deposits in a bank account. Under stress, they behave very differently. Wage income depends on labor staying in motion. Ownership income depends on assets continuing to produce value through rent, dividends, royalties, or business profits.

That difference helps explain why some people panic during downturns while others stay relatively composed. The gap usually has less to do with intelligence than structure. People respond to the financial system they live inside. If every expense in your life depends on wages and asset prices staying high, volatility feels personal very quickly.

Financial markets amplify this feeling because prices move faster than businesses do. A stock can fall 8 percent in a day because investors become worried about the future. The business behind that stock may still be selling drinks, processing payments, shipping packages, or collecting subscriptions at almost the same pace as the week before. Markets price expectations. Businesses continue operating in real time.

That is why ownership income deserves more attention than it usually receives. When you own a productive asset, you are connected to ongoing economic activity, not just a quoted price. A customer buys a Coca-Cola at a gas station in Ohio. Another uses an American Express card to pay for dinner in Dallas. Those purchases flow through large businesses with stable profit streams, and a portion of those profits can eventually reach shareholders.

Warren Buffett offers a good illustration because his public image often centers on buying great companies and holding them for decades. That is true as far as it goes, though the deeper advantage is easier to miss. Berkshire Hathaway owns businesses and stock positions that regularly send cash back to the company. Buffett does not simply wait for prices to rise. He gets paid while he waits.

Coca-Cola shows the mechanism clearly. Berkshire Hathaway owns roughly 400 million shares of the company, and Coca-Cola has paid regular dividends for decades. With an annual dividend above $1.80 per share in recent years, that single holding can produce close to $700 million in annual cash income for Berkshire. Every quarter, money arrives because people around the world continue buying a familiar product.

American Express works in a similar way. Berkshire owns a large stake in the company, and American Express distributes dividends from the profits generated by card fees, transaction activity, and financial services. Each swipe by a customer has a long chain of participants behind it, and one of those participants is the long-term owner collecting a share of the economics. Ownership turns ordinary commerce into recurring personal income.

That is a very different experience from relying only on price appreciation. If your plan depends entirely on someone paying more for your asset later, you live closer to the mood of the market. If your asset produces income along the way, you live closer to the output of the asset itself. The first condition creates more urgency. The second creates more patience.

Psychology helps explain why this matters so much. Daniel Kahneman and Amos Tversky showed that people feel losses more intensely than gains of the same size. A decline of $10,000 usually hurts more than a gain of $10,000 feels good. Once that idea appears on a brokerage screen, it becomes easy to understand why investors suddenly want to act. Loss aversion becomes especially powerful when savings are carrying too much weight. If the same account is supposed to fund retirement, absorb emergencies, and provide a sense of safety, any decline will feel larger than the numbers alone suggest. The person is responding to risk, though also to the possibility of losing options. Selling becomes emotionally attractive because it seems to restore control.

Cashflow changes that emotional equation by introducing another signal. A dividend arriving in the account says the asset is still producing. Rent paid on time says the property is still functioning. A business distribution says customers are still buying. Those signals do not erase volatility, though they do reduce the feeling that everything has suddenly stopped working.

That reduction in pressure is one of the least discussed advantages in investing. People often talk about return, valuation, and timing. They spend less time on the emotional cost of needing their assets to behave well every single month. Cashflow lowers that cost because it gives the owner something valuable during the waiting period. It gives them income, and income buys time.

Time is a central force in investing because most durable wealth compounds slowly. Businesses grow over years. Dividends are reinvested quarter by quarter.

Real estate becomes more useful when occupancy remains stable over long stretches. The person who can stay in the game usually has a better chance than the person who must keep interrupting the process to meet immediate needs. That is why the difference between working and owning is so important. Working gives you income only while your labor remains active. Owning gives you access to income generated by assets that continue working whether you are present or asleep. The first model ties money tightly to your calendar. The second begins loosening that connection.

This does not mean labor income lacks value. For most people, wages provide the starting point for everything that follows. A paycheck pays rent, covers food, funds savings, and allows the first investment to happen at all. Labor is where most financial journeys begin. The key shift occurs when part of that labor income is converted into assets that can start sending money back.

Rental real estate offers one familiar example. A tenant pays for the use of a home each month, and part of that payment goes to the owner. The owner may still deal with repairs, vacancies, taxes, and insurance, though the financial logic remains simple. The property is producing recurring income because it serves an ongoing need. Dividend-paying stocks follow the same logic on a different scale. A shareholder may own a tiny slice of a company with factories, software systems, retail stores, or payment networks spread across many places at once. The owner does not manage those systems directly. The owner receives a share of the profits because ownership itself establishes the claim.

Royalties make the idea even easier to see. A songwriter can do the work once and continue receiving income when the song is streamed, played publicly, or licensed later. The effort happened in the past. The cashflow continues in the present. Ownership stretches the economic life of labor.

What matters across all these examples is the behavior they produce. Recurring income makes expenses easier to carry. It reduces the pressure to sell during downturns. It lets a household think further ahead because every financial decision no longer depends on wages alone. Once that shift begins, volatility starts to feel less like a threat to survival and more like a condition of participation.

This is the deeper meaning of cashflow. It changes how an investor behaves because it changes what an investor depends on. Someone who owns productive assets still experiences uncertainty, though they experience it with a cushion. The cushion is not comfort in the abstract. It is income arriving while the future sorts itself out. That is the bridge between working and owning. Work gives you the means to begin. Ownership gives you a way to continue with more stability. Cashflow sits in the middle of that transition, and it is what makes patience financially possible.

The Quiet Power of Boring Assets

A strange thing happens when you study people and institutions that stay wealthy for a very long time. Their systems often look unimpressive from the outside. They do not depend on constant excitement, heroic timing, or lucky bursts of momentum. They depend on income that repeats, on contracts that hold, and on assets that keep doing their job long after the owner has stopped paying attention.

That quiet repetition receives very little public attention. Financial media prefers movement because movement is easy to dramatize. A stock that doubles in six months becomes a story. A cryptocurrency that surges over a weekend becomes a story. A company that sends rent checks, royalty payments, or dividends year after year usually does not become a story, even when that pattern is doing far more to build durable wealth.

This is one reason people misunderstand how many fortunes are actually built. The public tends to notice the visible business and miss the asset underneath it. We see the restaurant, the product, the celebrity founder, the stock chart. We spend less time looking at the contract, the land, the lease, the royalty agreement, or the dividend policy. Yet those quieter structures are often where the stability lives.

McDonald's offers a useful example because almost everyone thinks they know what business it is in. It sells burgers, fries, and soft drinks through more than 40,000 locations around the world. That is the visible business, and it is a large one. The less visible business is the one that matters more for this chapter: McDonald's has long owned or controlled much of the real estate beneath those restaurants and leased it to franchise operators.

That detail changes the way the company looks. A franchisee opens the restaurant, hires the workers, orders the food, and handles the daily grind of serving customers. McDonald's, sitting above that activity, collects rent and royalties from the operator using its land, buildings, and brand. The restaurant produces motion. The real estate produces recurring income. This distinction explains why the company has been so durable. Rent arrives on a schedule. Royalties arrive on a schedule. The corporation does not need a viral moment to make the model work. It needs thousands of operators opening their doors each morning and paying for the privilege of using a system built on top of owned assets. Stability comes from ownership tied to repetition.

That same logic appears everywhere once you know how to look for it. A small business owner who has built dependable systems receives profit because the enterprise continues serving people after the original setup work is done. The asset class matters less than people think. The behavior matters more. Does the asset send income back to the owner on a reasonably predictable basis? Does it remain tied to some ongoing human need, habit, or use? Does it continue producing without requiring the owner to rebuild the machine every morning? Those questions reveal more than the label attached to the asset.

This is why boring assets deserve more respect than they usually receive. They produce a kind of progress that feels almost too ordinary to celebrate. A dividend lands in the account. Rent arrives on the first of the month. A business distribution shows up at quarter-end. None of these events looks dramatic on social media. Each one quietly changes the owner's life.

Most people skip over this stage because human attention is drawn toward speed. Fast gains carry emotional force. They create stories people want to repeat. Someone doubles their money in a hot stock, catches a crypto run at the right moment, or flips a property into a higher market, and the whole episode feels cinematic. Predictable income, by comparison, feels slow because it asks the owner to appreciate reliability before excitement.

That preference for excitement has a cost. Assets purchased for a quick win often depend heavily on mood, timing, and favorable market conditions. Income-producing assets depend more on continued use. A tenant needs shelter. A customer buys a product again. A business keeps serving a market it understands. This is a less glamorous relationship with money, though it is often a more durable one.

The deeper advantage of boring assets appears in the way they shape behavior. A person receiving recurring income begins to experience financial life differently, even when the amount is still modest. The first few hundred dollars a month may cover groceries, utilities, or part of an insurance bill. The amount may be small in absolute terms, though its effect on the mind can be surprisingly large.

Predictability changes the texture of a household budget. Expenses that once leaned entirely on labor income now have another support beneath them. Decisions stop feeling so tightly linked to the next paycheck. The owner begins to look at time differently because some part of monthly survival has been assigned to an asset instead of a work schedule.

This is why recurring income can feel more valuable than a larger pile of idle savings. A person with $500,000 sitting passively in cash may still feel exposed if that money produces little ongoing support. A person with a smaller asset base that reliably sends income each month may feel calmer because the structure itself is carrying part of the load. In daily life, reliability often matters more than headline size.

Cashflow creates that patience because it does three practical things at once. It helps pay recurring bills. It reduces emotional pressure during periods of volatility. It gives the owner more room to think in years instead of days. Once those conditions are in place, better investment behavior becomes much more likely.

Cash Flow as the Engine of the CAPL System

A useful way to understand the CAPL system is to begin with a failed version of it. During the housing boom of the early 2000s, many investors believed they had found an easy formula for wealth. Buy a property, wait a year, refinance, and watch the value climb. The math looked convincing while prices were rising, which is exactly why so many people missed the weakness in the structure.

By 2006, that weakness was sitting in plain view across parts of the United States. In cities such as Phoenix, Las Vegas, Miami, and parts of inland California, homes were being purchased with very little margin for error. Investors were counting on appreciation to do the heavy lifting. Rental income often mattered less than the assumption that someone else would soon pay more.

That assumption felt reasonable for a while because the numbers kept cooperating. According to Federal Housing Finance Agency data, the national median home price rose more than 60 percent between 2000 and 2006. In hotter local markets, the gains were even larger. A property could look brilliant on paper even when the monthly cash flow was weak, because rising prices were covering the flaws.

This is where the difference between appreciation and cashflow becomes decisive. Appreciation can make you look wealthy. Cash flow helps you stay solvent. Those are related ideas, though they behave very differently once conditions become difficult. During the boom, many investors treated the first as if it were enough. They bought properties with adjustable-rate mortgages, thin down payments, and rental income that barely covered the carrying costs. Some accepted negative cashflow because they believed future price gains would erase present strain. In that world, patience was never really patience. It was dependent on a rising market.

When housing prices began rolling over in 2007, the weakness surfaced quickly. By the time the financial crisis deepened, the S&P Case-Shiller National Home Price Index had fallen roughly 27 percent from its peak. A property that looked safe at a rising valuation suddenly had to justify itself using rents, expenses, debt service, taxes, and maintenance. Many could not.

When the story around an asset fades, what remains? In real estate, what remained was a monthly bill. Mortgage payments still arrived. Property taxes still arrived. Repairs still arrived. If the rent was too low to cover those obligations, the owner had not purchased a durable investment. The owner had purchased a rising price with a house attached to it.

This was the hidden fragility of many 2008-era investments. They depended on appreciation for survival, not only for profit. Once prices stopped rising, refinancing became harder, buyers disappeared, and the monthly economics turned against the owner. Between 2007 and 2010, millions of American homes entered foreclosure proceedings because debt kept moving while the original thesis no longer worked.

That history explains why cashflow sits at the front of the CAPL framework. Cashflow is not the reward you collect after the system succeeds. It is the condition that lets the system keep functioning when markets become less cooperative. It pays the carrying cost of time. This is also why cashflow and appreciation should never be treated as interchangeable. Appreciation expands net worth over long periods, which makes it essential to building real wealth. Cashflow does a different job. It covers expenses, absorbs shocks, and keeps the owner from having to liquidate assets at the worst moment. One builds value. The other protects continuity.

The order matters because continuity is what gives growth a chance. An investor who owns productive assets with recurring income can hold through ugly periods without turning every downturn into a personal emergency. An investor who depends only on asset prices must hope the market stays generous. Hope is a poor substitute for structure.

This leads directly back to the logic of CAPL. Cashflow comes first because cashflow funds appreciation. Income from a rental property, dividend portfolio, business distribution, or royalty stream can be redirected into assets that rise in value over time. That is how the system begins to reinforce itself. The owner is no longer waiting for a single asset to save them. The owner is using one stream of income to acquire another source of future strength.

Investors often make three mistakes at this stage, and each one reveals a misunderstanding of what cashflow is for. Some use too much leverage before their income base is stable, which turns a useful tool into a source of pressure. Some chase yields that look attractive on paper though rest on shaky businesses or fragile market conditions. Others spend every dollar of new cashflow as lifestyle income and quietly stop the compounding process before it has a chance to gather force.

The pattern underneath these mistakes is simple. Cashflow feels rewarding, so people treat it like the finish line. In this framework, it plays a different role. Cashflow is the engine. It is supposed to keep feeding the system. That is what creates the compounding loop. Income from existing assets buys additional assets. Those assets begin producing their own income. The expanded income base creates more choices, more resilience, and a wider margin for patient decisions. Over time, the system becomes stronger because each cycle adds another layer of support beneath the next one.

The most valuable effect of this process is often psychological before it is visible on a spreadsheet. Recurring income reduces the strain that pushes people into rushed decisions. It becomes easier to evaluate risk calmly, easier to hold quality assets through volatility, and easier to wait for opportunities that deserve capital. The investor begins behaving like someone with time on their side because, in a practical sense, they do.

So, where should you start in your situation?

Start by looking carefully at how money currently enters your life. For most people, nearly every dollar arrives through work performed during the same week or month. That arrangement works as long as employment remains stable and health allows continued effort. The CAPL approach asks you to begin shifting that structure gradually by converting a portion of labor income into assets that can produce income on their own.

The next step involves choosing assets that are capable of sending money back to you while you hold them. These assets often appear less exciting than speculative opportunities, which explains why they receive less attention in financial conversations. Rental properties, dividend-producing businesses, small enterprises, and royalty-producing intellectual property all share the same financial behavior. They convert ongoing economic activity into recurring income for the owner. Identify these ones.

Early cashflow streams often begin at a scale that feels modest. A dividend portfolio might produce several hundred dollars during the first year. A small rental property may generate a narrow margin above its expenses during the early stages of ownership. Those amounts can seem insignificant compared with the cost of living, though their true value lies in the change they create inside your financial structure.

Once income begins arriving from assets, a subtle decision begins shaping the future of the system. Recurring payments naturally invite spending because they feel like rewards for good financial decisions. The CAPL framework treats those payments differently. That's what we'll cover in the next chapter.

For now, remember that the process unfolds slowly at the beginning. A few small income streams rarely transform financial life overnight. Yet each stream reduces dependence on wages and adds another layer of resilience beneath your household budget. Over enough years, those layers create the stability that allows appreciation and long-term investing to work with far less pressure.

FREE GIFT: Watch The full CAPL+DR System Training

You just covered a powerful concept. And here's the truth information alone doesn't change your life. Execution does. So I created something for you. I put together a step-by-step video training where I walk you through exactly how to apply everything youjust learned, and take it even further. You can watch it for free. No opt in. No catch. Just scan the QR code or go to https://3twarrioracademy.com/training-capldr

SCAN ME

CHAPTER 12

APPRECIATION - TURNING CASH FLOW INTO GROWTH

Most people can identify the month when money stopped feeling slippery. The bills arrived, the paycheck arrived, and for once the two did not seem to be chasing each other around the calendar. A small amount stayed behind after the essentials were covered, and that small remainder felt larger than its dollar value because it suggested a new kind of control.

Marvin reaches that point in his early thirties. His work has become steady, his expenses have become predictable, and the low-grade financial chaos of his twenties has begun to recede. At the end of most months, about five hundred dollars remains after rent, food, transportation, and the usual obligations have been handled. He does what careful people usually do. He moves the extra cash into savings, then repeats the process the next month and the month after that. By the end of the first year he has about six thousand dollars, and a few years later the number has crossed twenty thousand, which feels responsible, adult, and reassuring.

Then a quieter feeling appears. The balance is larger, yet his financial life does not feel much larger. Marvin is safer than he was before, though he does not yet feel meaningfully further ahead.

That tension matters because it captures a moment many people recognize and struggle to name. Saving money changes your margin for error, which is deeply valuable, though it does not automatically change your relationship with the future. The account provides protection, and protection is only the first job money can perform.

So what should happen once stability arrives?

The answer begins with a simple distinction. Some money is held for safety, and some money is put to work through ownership. The first kind helps you survive surprises. The second kind helps you participate in growth.

A savings account performs an essential function because life remains unpredictable even for disciplined households. Cars break down, jobs change, roofs leak, and medical bills arrive on their own schedule. Cash reserves matter because they create breathing room when ordinary life becomes expensive without warning. That role, however, has limits. Cash stored in an account remains mostly where it is. The balance can rise through regular deposits and modest interest, though the money itself is not deeply connected to the forces that make economies expand.

Ownership works differently. When money buys a piece of land, a share of a business, or an asset with durable scarcity, it joins a larger story already unfolding in the world. Population grows, companies improve, demand rises, and the value of certain assets rises with those changes.

That gradual rise is what we call appreciation.

The idea sounds abstract until it is placed beside ordinary experience. Marvin's savings account feels safe because the number is visible and stable. An appreciating asset behaves differently because its value depends on what is happening around it, not just on the balance printed on a statement.

A city can become more valuable because more people want to live and work there. A business can become more valuable because it serves more customers with better products and greater efficiency. A scarce asset can become more valuable because supply grows slowly while demand keeps rising.

Once you see that pattern, an important shift begins. Money can either sit inside the economy or own a piece of it. That is the threshold Marvin is approaching, even if he does not yet have language for it.

History makes the point clearer because the pattern has repeated for generations. In the early twentieth century, Americans could buy shares in a wide range of public companies operating inside an economy that was industrializing, urbanizing, and growing more productive over time. Railroads moved goods, manufacturers expanded output, and consumer businesses sold to a country becoming larger and more connected each decade. A share of stock represented partial ownership in that process. It was not simply a claim on a ticker symbol or a line on a brokerage statement. It was a claim on the future earnings of a business trying to serve a growing market.

Over long periods, that distinction turned out to matter enormously. Historical market data shows that a diversified portfolio of large American companies has produced average annual returns in roughly the 9 to 10 percent range across many decades, though the path included recessions, bear markets, inflation shocks, and war. The journey was uneven. The direction was durable.

That long record reveals something easy to miss in daily life. A dollar placed into productive ownership in the 1920s did not grow because the investor was unusually brilliant or unusually busy. It grew because the underlying businesses kept working, producing, adapting, and selling into an expanding economy. Factories improved output. Engineers developed new products. Managers opened new markets. Customers kept buying. Owners participated in those efforts because ownership linked their money to productive activity.

This is one of the quiet dividing lines in finance. Income is usually tied to your labor. Appreciation is tied to what your money owns. The distinction helps explain why stability can feel incomplete. Marvin has already improved the part of life governed by discipline and budgeting. He has reduced financial friction and created surplus. What he has not yet done is connect that surplus to systems that can grow without requiring more hours from him.

That is where appreciation enters the picture. The challenge is that appreciation rarely announces itself early. A raise changes the next paycheck, and the effect is immediate. Investment growth is slower, less visible, and more dependent on time, which makes it easy to underestimate in its early stages.

Compounding deepens that effect. The first gains are small because the base is small, which makes the process feel underwhelming just when it most needs patience. Years later, those early gains begin generating gains of their own, and the pattern that once looked trivial starts to look powerful. This is why many people feel emotionally unconvinced by good investing when they first encounter it. The logic is clear, though the experience is quiet. Appreciation often looks dull before it looks impressive.

Marvin's savings account is outside that process. It preserves value, adds a little interest, and waits for instructions. If part of his monthly surplus begins purchasing appreciating assets, the role of that money changes from storage to participation.

That change sounds small, although it is structural. The same five hundred dollars that once existed only as a cushion can begin acquiring shares in businesses, exposure to productive land, or ownership in assets that rise with growing demand. The amount has not changed. The assignment has.

This is the point where many of you will begin to feel the argument, because it touches a common frustration. People can become more responsible for years without becoming much wealthier. They reduce waste, pay on time, and slowly build savings, yet the larger financial horizon remains stubbornly far away.

The reason is often simple. Responsibility creates stability. Ownership creates growth.

Once that sentence lands, another issue comes into view. If appreciation is so powerful, why do so many people fail to stay with it long enough to benefit?

When markets fall, many investors experience the decline as a personal warning rather than a normal feature of long-term ownership. They step away, wait for reassurance, and return after recovery is already underway. Historical fund flow data has shown versions of this pattern for years: money often leaves after declines and returns after rallies. That reaction breaks the very process appreciation depends on. Long-term returns come from remaining connected to productive assets across full cycles, which means enduring the periods when ownership feels least comfortable. Patience matters here for a practical reason, not a moral one.

This is where cashflow becomes more than a budgeting concept. Reliable income allows a person to hold appreciating assets without depending on their immediate sale for monthly survival. Bills can still be paid while markets move, which gives time a chance to do its work. Cashflow does more than relieve pressure. It creates the emotional and practical room required to become an owner. Without that room, every market swing feels urgent. With it, temporary declines become easier to survive and easier to ignore.

Marvin's extra five hundred dollars therefore carries a larger meaning than it first appears to. It is a monthly sign that survival is no longer consuming every available dollar. It is also the first unit of capital available for ownership.

That change alters the way progress should be measured. Most people begin by asking how much money they have saved, which is a reasonable question during the stability phase. A more powerful question emerges once surplus exists: what does that money own?

The difference between those questions is the difference between storage and participation. One measures how much value has been set aside. The other measures whether that value has been connected to growth.

Over time, this shift becomes visible in the structure of a person's life. Surplus income buys assets. Those assets rise in value as businesses expand, cities develop, and demand grows around scarce resources. The gains can then remain invested, which allows compounding to build on a larger base. Nothing dramatic has to happen for this to work. The process is often quiet, repetitive, and almost boring from the inside. That is part of its strength because wealth usually grows more like a routine than an event.

Marvin has not changed careers, launched a company, or discovered an exotic strategy. He has simply reached the point where money can begin doing a second job. One part still protects the present. Another part can begin purchasing the future.

That is the moment when stability becomes growth, and it is a real change in financial position.

Why Certain Assets Keep Rising

Once appreciation makes sense, a more interesting question usually appears right behind it. Why does one asset keep climbing for decades while another drifts, stalls, or simply sits there? People often answer that question with personality stories about genius, timing, or unusual insight, though the deeper explanation is usually more structural.

The assets that rise most reliably tend to be attached to one of two forces. They either belong to systems that keep expanding, or they are limited in supply while demand keeps building around them. In the strongest cases, both forces are present at the same time. That is why appreciation can look mysterious from a distance and almost obvious up close. The mystery comes from price. The explanation comes from context. Once you see the surrounding system, the movement in value begins to make more sense.

Manhattan offers one of the clearest examples in American economic history. Two hundred years ago, much of the island looked ordinary. There were farms, scattered homes, undeveloped land, and long stretches that gave very little hint of what would later stand there.

The grid plan adopted in 1807 matters for that reason. It organized space long before the full demand for that space existed, which meant the island's future was being quietly prepared while much of it still looked rural. At the time, land values remained modest because the larger machine around Manhattan had not fully arrived yet.

Then the machine arrived. New York grew into a port city, then a commercial center, then a financial center, then a global center of culture and capital. Railroads connected it to the rest of the country, shipping channels connected it to the world, and Wall Street gave it a central role in the movement of money itself. The number of people competing to live, work, and build there kept rising. The scale of that growth was enormous. In 1800, New York City had roughly 60,000 residents. By 1900, the population had moved past 3 million. That is what appreciation often looks like in real life: an asset stays physically the same while the world around it changes completely.

Manhattan's land did not become more valuable because the island learned a new skill. It became more valuable because demand crowded into a fixed space. The rivers did not move, the island did not widen, and the amount of land available did not expand to match the rising intensity of commerce, immigration, finance, and urban life.

That is the mechanism. Growth increases demand. Scarcity limits supply. Price responds to the gap between the two.

Once you understand Manhattan, a great deal of real estate becomes easier to read. The same pattern appears in central London, in parts of Hong Kong, in San Francisco, and in neighborhoods of major cities that become magnets for talent and capital. In each case, people are competing for something that cannot easily multiply.

Land makes the lesson visible because it is easy to picture. Businesses teach the same lesson in a less physical form. A good company can appreciate for the same reason a good piece of urban land can appreciate: it sits inside an expanding system and captures some portion of that expansion.

This is what early shareholders in companies like Apple and Microsoft were really buying, even if they did not fully realize it at the time. They were buying partial ownership in businesses positioned inside a market that was about to become much larger than it looked. Personal computing in the late 1970s and early 1980s still felt specialized, technical, and uncertain. The market was young, and the future size of that market was difficult to see clearly.

Yet the underlying direction was already there. More offices were using computers. More households were beginning to adopt them. Software was becoming essential, and the computer was slowly shifting from a specialized tool into a mainstream platform for work, communication, and entertainment. That shift mattered more than any quarterly number. As computing spread, the companies building the hardware, software, and operating systems around that shift gained access to a larger and larger market. Apple and Microsoft grew because the world they served kept widening.

Shareholders who held their ownership over long stretches benefited from that widening. They did not need to predict every product cycle or every market correction. They needed to remain attached to a business that was participating in a durable expansion. That is a useful way to think about stock ownership. A share is a small claim on future demand. If the business keeps finding ways to serve a growing market profitably, the value of that claim tends to rise over time.

Real estate and businesses therefore teach the same lesson from different angles. In Manhattan, the scarce thing was land in a location the world increasingly wanted. In Apple or Microsoft, the scarce thing was productive ownership in companies serving a market that kept expanding across decades.

Some assets rise for a different reason. Their value depends less on an expanding business or a growing city and more on the discipline of limited supply. Gold is the classic example because it has carried this role across centuries and across civilizations.

Gold does not produce cashflow, build software, or collect rent. Its long-term attraction comes from rarity, durability, and the fact that new supply enters the world slowly. Mining is difficult, time-consuming, and expensive, which places a natural brake on how quickly total supply can grow. That slow supply growth matters when demand changes. If investors, central banks, or households decide they want more gold, supply cannot suddenly surge to meet that desire. Prices therefore adjust through the only mechanism available, which is a higher value placed on the existing stock.

Bitcoin introduced a modern version of the same principle. The scarcity is digital rather than geological, though the logic is familiar. The system is designed so that no more than 21 million coins will ever exist, and that rule gives the asset its core economic identity. The importance of that design becomes clearer when adoption increases. As more people, institutions, and firms decide they want exposure to Bitcoin, they are competing for a supply that does not expand in response to higher demand. The supply rule stays fixed. Price absorbs the pressure.

Gold and Bitcoin are different assets serving different investors, though they are linked by the same deeper idea. In both cases, appreciation can emerge because demand grows around something whose supply remains constrained. Scarcity, when it is credible, becomes economically powerful.

This is the broader pattern you need to see. Appreciating assets usually have one of two advantages, and sometimes both. They are connected to a system that is growing, or they possess a form of scarcity that demand cannot easily dissolve. An asset with no meaningful growth around it and no real scarcity supporting it has very little to pull on its value. It may remain useful. It may even remain expensive. It usually struggles to compound.

Once you understand that, investing begins to feel less like prediction and more like selection. The goal is not to guess tomorrow's headline or chase whatever looks exciting in the current cycle. The goal is to place surplus cashflow into assets that participate in durable forces already shaping the economy.

Those forces are often hiding in plain sight. Cities keep attracting talent and capital. Technologies keep changing how people live and work. Networks keep expanding. Some forms of scarcity keep holding because supply really is limited. Appreciation follows those conditions more often than it follows excitement. This is also why appreciation can feel slow at first. Growth and scarcity do their work gradually, then visibly, then decisively. For a long stretch, the gain may look almost uneventful. Over time, the cumulative effect becomes easier to see because the underlying forces never stopped operating.

The practical implication is straightforward. Surplus income becomes more powerful when it is consistently directed toward assets with a reason to rise. That reason usually lives in growth, scarcity, or the meeting point between the two. Once you see that pattern, the logic of appreciation becomes far more stable.

Where Appreciation Begins

Understanding appreciation eventually leads to a practical moment of hesitation. The idea makes sense in theory, though many people still pause when the conversation turns to action. The question becomes simple and uncomfortable at the same time: where does someone actually begin?

Most people assume the answer involves complicated strategies, insider knowledge, or a perfectly timed opportunity. Financial headlines often reinforce that impression because the news tends to highlight dramatic gains, sudden crashes, and investors who appear to move with uncanny precision.

Yet the real beginning tends to look much quieter. The first step usually involves something ordinary: converting consistent surplus income into consistent ownership. That shift does not require unusual timing, and it rarely depends on discovering a rare opportunity. It depends mainly on participation. The previous chapter focused on cashflow for exactly this reason. Stable income creates room to think beyond immediate expenses, which means money can begin serving more than one purpose. Some funds remain available for daily life and unexpected problems, while surplus funds become available for ownership.

This transition marks the practical starting point for appreciation.

Consider Marvin again. His finances now leave roughly five hundred dollars available at the end of most months after the essential expenses of living have been handled. The number feels modest relative to the scale of global markets, though its importance lies in consistency rather than size. Five hundred dollars arriving regularly becomes something different from five hundred dollars appearing occasionally. Regular participation turns a small surplus into a steady stream of ownership, and ownership accumulates quietly over time.

One common way people begin is through diversified investment funds that hold shares in hundreds of companies. These funds allow individuals to participate in a wide collection of businesses that operate across industries, regions, and economic cycles.

This structure spreads ownership broadly across the economy rather than concentrating it in a single company or sector. Some businesses inevitably struggle or disappear as markets evolve, while others expand and replace them. The investor participates in the combined outcome of many enterprises rather than the fate of one. Historical evidence supports this approach because diversified equity markets have grown alongside expanding economies. As productivity rises, industries evolve, and populations increase, businesses that adapt and innovate tend to become more valuable over time.

Ownership in those businesses therefore participates in the broader progress of the economy.

Real estate offers another path that reflects the same principle from a different angle. Property located in areas experiencing population growth or economic development becomes connected to rising demand for housing, offices, and commercial space.

Cities illustrate this dynamic repeatedly across decades. When employment opportunities expand in a region and infrastructure improves, more people arrive seeking work and stability. Housing demand rises, businesses follow the population, and land values often respond to the increasing competition for space. Property owners who hold assets in such environments participate in that expansion. Rent payments may provide ongoing income while the underlying value of the land responds to long-term changes in the surrounding economy.

Each category of asset operates under slightly different conditions, though the underlying logic remains consistent. Surplus cashflow gradually acquires ownership in systems where demand has room to grow or supply remains constrained. The challenge many people encounter at this stage involves timing. Market headlines frequently focus on peaks, corrections, and moments when investors appear to move with perfect precision. That coverage creates the impression that successful investing requires entering the market at exactly the right moment.

Long-term evidence suggests a quieter approach. A method known as dollar-cost averaging allows investors to participate steadily without attempting to predict short-term market movements. Instead of waiting for ideal conditions, a fixed amount of money is invested at regular intervals, often monthly. This approach produces a simple pattern. When prices fall, the same investment purchases more shares. When prices rise, the same investment purchases fewer shares. Over time the investor accumulates ownership across a wide range of market conditions.

The strategy converts investing from a prediction problem into a participation habit.

Behavioral finance research suggests that consistent investing also reduces the emotional pressure associated with market fluctuations. Automatic contributions remove the temptation to delay decisions while waiting for perfect clarity, which rarely appears in financial markets.

Consistency therefore becomes a practical advantage. Cashflow once again plays a central role in supporting that consistency. Regular income allows investments to occur without disrupting daily life or creating financial strain. Each month's surplus becomes another small acquisition of ownership.

Over time those acquisitions accumulate. Imagine Marvin continuing to invest his five hundred dollar surplus each month into diversified assets. After ten years he would have contributed sixty thousand dollars, and the total value of those investments could exceed that figure depending on market conditions during the period. Extend the timeline to twenty or thirty years and the compounding effect becomes easier to see. Contributions continue, investment returns accumulate, and the base from which those returns grow becomes steadily larger.

The pattern rarely unfolds dramatically in its early years. Initial progress may feel slow because the investment base remains small and market movements fluctuate from year to year. Patience therefore becomes part of the process.

What gradually changes is the structure of Marvin's financial life. His income continues providing stability and covering daily expenses, while his assets begin participating in broader economic growth. Businesses expand, cities develop, and the value of ownership responds to those forces.

Over time the relationship between income and assets begins to shift. Assets contribute more to financial progress because appreciation and reinvestment compound across long periods.

The transformation often feels quiet from the inside. Each monthly contribution appears small, and market fluctuations sometimes obscure the steady accumulation happening beneath the surface.

Eventually the effect becomes visible. The asset base grows large enough that appreciation itself begins contributing meaningfully to overall wealth. At that point ownership joins income as an important driver of financial progress.

This stage introduces a new responsibility. Assets that rise in value eventually require protection because markets move in cycles. Periods of strong growth tend to alternate with corrections, slowdowns, and unexpected disruptions that challenge even experienced investors. Understanding appreciation therefore leads naturally to the next stage of the framework. Cashflow created the foundation. Appreciation converted surplus income into expanding ownership. The next task involves protecting the value that ownership creates as economic conditions continue changing.

FREE GIFT: Watch The full CAPL+DR System Training

You just covered a powerful concept. And here's the truth information alone doesn't change your life. Execution does. So I created something for you. I put together a step-by-step video training where I walk you through exactly how to apply everything youjust learned, and take it even further. You can watch it for free. No opt in. No catch. Just scan the QR code or go to https://3twarrioracademy.com/training-capldr

SCAN ME

CHAPTER 13

PROTECTION - SAFEGUARDING YOUR GAINS

In 1988, Yellowstone National Park burned on a scale few people expected. By the time the fires ended, roughly 1.2 million acres across the greater Yellowstone area had burned, including large portions of the park itself. For many Americans, the event looked like a failure of nature or a failure of management. It looked sudden. It looked extreme. It looked like a disaster that arrived from the outside.

The deeper story had been building for decades. For much of the twentieth century, the Park Service followed a simple policy: put out fires quickly. Small fires were treated as threats to be suppressed, because suppression felt responsible and orderly. A forest with fewer fires seemed safer than a forest with more fires, and that assumption guided policy for years. The logic made sense on paper, which is often how fragile systems first earn our trust.

The problem was that forests do not remain still while managers are making decisions. Dead wood accumulated on the ground. Underbrush thickened. Smaller burns that might have cleared fuel from the system disappeared, and the landscape grew denser with each passing season. What looked stable from year to year was quietly becoming more combustible over time, because the visible calm concealed a growing concentration of risk.

When lightning strikes and dry conditions arrived in the summer of 1988, the result was less surprising to fire ecologists than it was to the broader public. Yellowstone had not become dangerous in a single season. It had become dangerous through a long stretch of apparent safety that allowed hidden fuel to build. The fires were dramatic, but the real story lay in the years before the flames, when the conditions for a larger collapse were being assembled in plain sight.

That pattern shows up in financial life more often than people realize. Long stretches of rising markets create a similar kind of calm, where gains accumulate, confidence rises, and the system starts to look sturdier than it is. The danger appears later, after success has already been rewarded and after exposure has already grown. By the time the break arrives, the issue often looks like volatility, though the deeper issue is that stability was misunderstood.

Protection begins with that recognition. Some systems fail because they are left exposed. Others fail because their defenses are built around the wrong problem. An investor can spend years focused on growth, diversification, tax efficiency, and returns, while overlooking the simpler question of what happens when conditions turn and the portfolio has to absorb stress rather than enjoy momentum. That question matters because financial setbacks rarely arrive as abstractions. They arrive when assets fall, when liquidity tightens, and when people discover that yesterday's confidence had very little cushioning underneath it.

This is why two investors can live through the same downturn and emerge with entirely different outcomes. One is forced into damage control. The other remains patient and intact. The difference often has little to do with intelligence, forecasting skill, or effort. It has to do with protection, which becomes visible only when the environment stops cooperating.

The most dangerous stage in investing often arrives after things have gone well for a while. Early in the process, most people understand they are still building and still learning, so caution feels natural. Later, after appreciation has done its work and balances have grown, the emotional atmosphere changes. Gains begin to feel familiar, the path starts to look dependable, and the mind slowly converts recent experience into future expectation.

A portfolio worth $10,000 that falls 20 percent creates disappointment and a useful lesson in volatility. A portfolio worth $1 million that falls 20 percent removes $200,000 and changes how a household thinks about plans, security, and timing. The percentage remains the same, though the psychological and practical consequences expand with the size of the base. Growth increases opportunity, and it also increases exposure.

This is one of the quieter features of wealth accumulation. The more you build, the more there is to protect. People often associate vulnerability with having too little, because scarcity is easy to see and easy to feel. Exposure can grow on the other side as well, especially when rising values create the impression that the system is becoming safer as it becomes larger. In practice, larger positions can produce a different kind of fragility, because more capital is now attached to the same swings in sentiment, valuation, and liquidity.

Investors become more confident in what they own, because recent results offer emotional evidence that the strategy is working. Markets become more crowded for the same reason. Assets that have risen attract attention, capital, and imitation, which can push prices higher while making the structure underneath them more delicate. What makes this dangerous is not enthusiasm by itself. What makes it dangerous is that enthusiasm often arrives alongside declining sensitivity to loss.

History keeps returning to this point in different forms. Periods of expansion encourage the belief that growth is durable, and durable growth encourages looser habits around risk. Protection matters here because prosperity does not remove fragility. Prosperity can deepen it. Once gains become meaningful, the question changes from how to grow wealth to how to keep wealth from becoming vulnerable to the next turn in the cycle. That is where this chapter begins to do its real work.

Every generation seems to discover the same lesson in its own language. Prices rise for years, credit remains available, headlines grow more confident, and the public gradually adjusts to the idea that recent conditions reflect normal conditions. Then the cycle turns. What looked sturdy begins to look conditional, and what looked temporary in the buildup reveals itself as a recurring feature of financial history.

The past two centuries offer more than enough reminders. The stock market collapse of 1929 followed a period of heavy speculation and broad confidence in a new era of prosperity. The inflation crisis of the 1970s reshaped household budgets and investment assumptions after years in which many Americans had treated rising prices as a manageable background condition. The dot-com collapse in 2000 arrived after investors had convinced themselves that internet growth had changed the relationship between price and value. The financial crisis of 2008 emerged from a housing market that many households and institutions had come to view as fundamentally dependable. The pandemic shock of 2020 interrupted a long bull market with a speed that surprised even experienced professionals.

These episodes differed in cause, in scale, and in the assets they punished first. Some began with leverage, some with speculation, some with policy shifts, and some with external shocks. Yet the emotional pattern was remarkably consistent. Before each break, optimism had become familiar enough to feel rational. Risk was still present, though it had become harder to notice because rising prices made fragility easier to ignore.

This is where investors make a predictable mistake. They prepare carefully for growth because growth feels like the primary task. They learn how to earn, how to save, how to invest, and how to recognize opportunity in expanding markets. Far fewer prepare for interruption, even though interruption appears with impressive regularity once the lens widens beyond any single decade. Financial history contains long advances, sharp reversals, and recoveries that favor those who remained intact through the decline.

Markets do not move in straight lines. They move in cycles of expansion and contraction, and those cycles shape behavior long before they shape headlines. During expansion, confidence spreads faster than caution. During contraction, caution spreads faster than confidence. A person who understands this rhythm begins to see protection less as a defensive preference and more as an operating requirement inside a system that periodically resets expectations.

The cycle eventually reaches everyone, including disciplined households and thoughtful investors. The question is rarely whether disruption will return. The more practical question concerns how a person will respond when it does. Some people meet downturns with patience because their structure allows patience. Others meet the same downturns with urgency because their structure leaves little room for delay. That difference explains why survival in finance depends on more than absorbing losses on paper.

The deeper issue is compulsion. A downturn becomes more dangerous when it forces action before conditions improve, and financial history is full of people whose main mistake was timing they could no longer control. This is the point where protection stops being an abstract preference and starts to look like a condition for endurance within a cyclical system.

People often describe risk as the possibility of losing money, which is true in a narrow technical sense and incomplete in the way that matters most. A temporary decline in value can be recovered from if the owner has time, liquidity, and emotional room to wait. The more serious danger appears when a person loses the ability to choose the timing of their next move, because markets are often least forgiving at the exact moment someone is forced to respond.

That distinction becomes clear in ordinary life. A worker who loses employment during a recession may need to sell stocks after prices have already fallen. A household facing rising bills may liquidate investments to create short-term breathing room. A property owner with debt obligations may sell real estate into a weak market because the schedule of repayment refuses to wait for better conditions. In each case, the financial damage comes from pressure as much as from price movement, because pressure shortens the time available for judgment.

This is why protection deserves a larger role than most people give it. Protection creates time, and time changes the quality of every decision made during stress. An investor with reserves, stable buffers, or assets designed to hold value under pressure can remain still while others are rearranging plans around urgency. Remaining still can look passive from the outside, though in markets it is often a highly active advantage because it preserves choice when choice becomes scarce.

The best investors are rarely the people with the clearest predictions. They are the people who survive long enough for the future to reward them. That survival depends on structure more than brilliance, because periods of stress expose whether a portfolio was designed for volatility or designed only for progress. When progress pauses, the underlying design becomes visible.

Forced decisions also distort judgment in predictable ways. People under pressure reach for immediate relief, even when that relief damages long-term outcomes. They sell what is liquid, postpone what is strategic, and narrow their focus to the nearest obligation. None of this requires a lack of intelligence. It requires a lack of protection, because the absence of protection turns time into a luxury and patience into an unaffordable trait.

This is the quiet purpose of a protective layer. It reduces the chance that a temporary storm becomes a permanent financial setback by giving the investor more room to wait, assess, and preserve position. In that sense, protection creates the conditions under which good decisions remain available.

Protection becomes clearer once the idea is grounded in how investors actually organize their capital. When gains accumulate inside growth assets, a portion of those gains can be repositioned into holdings designed to behave differently during stress. The goal is structural balance rather than uniform exposure, because portfolios that rely on a single type of asset often experience the same type of risk at the same moment. Protection introduces variety in behavior so that every part of the portfolio does not respond to market conditions in the same way.

Appreciation increases value, though it also concentrates exposure inside the same environment that produced the gains. Protection changes that relationship by relocating some of the value into assets that operate under different pressures. The investor still participates in growth, though the portfolio now contains a layer designed to absorb volatility rather than amplify it.

Consider a homeowner who gradually expands a house over time, adding rooms, improving materials, and increasing the visible value of the structure. The expansion improves the home, though durability depends on the strength of the underlying structure that keeps the building stable when conditions change. Protection plays a similar role in finance because it strengthens the elements that help wealth endure stress rather than simply increasing its size.

This is why protection becomes most relevant after appreciation has already done its work. A rising market can produce significant gains across equities, property, private businesses, and digital assets. Those gains appear stable while markets remain cooperative, though they remain sensitive to the same forces that created them. Protection introduces separation by moving part of those gains into holdings whose function centers on stability rather than acceleration.

The practical result is that protection converts paper gains into more durable wealth. Gains recorded in account balances remain exposed while they stay concentrated in the same asset class or economic environment. Once part of those gains is transferred into defensive holdings, the investor holds a more stable financial position even while remaining invested in growth opportunities. The system becomes less dependent on a single market condition continuing indefinitely.

The tools used for protection have existed in different forms for centuries. Across cultures and economic systems, people have repeatedly sought ways to preserve purchasing power, maintain access to liquidity, and reduce the damage that accompanies periods of uncertainty. These efforts produced a set of financial tools that function primarily as stabilizers rather than accelerators inside a portfolio.

Protective assets usually fall into several broad categories that share the same underlying objective. Each category offers a different method of preserving value or maintaining stability when financial conditions become less predictable. Their structure and behavior vary, though their purpose remains aligned with the same principle: resilience during periods of stress.

One category includes precious metals such as gold and silver, which have historically served as stores of value during periods of monetary instability or declining currency confidence. During the inflation surge of the late 1970s, consumer prices in the United States rose at annual rates exceeding 10 percent in several years. Over roughly the same period, the price of gold moved from around $35 per ounce in the early 1970s to more than $800 by 1980. This pattern illustrates how certain assets respond differently when monetary conditions begin to shift.

Then we have the defensive financial instruments designed to hold value more steadily when broader markets experience turbulence. During the financial crisis of 2008, the S&P 500 declined by roughly 38 percent over the course of the year. Portfolios concentrated entirely in equities experienced the full impact of that decline, while portfolios that included stabilizing assets such as government bonds experienced smaller drawdowns. The difference influenced how quickly those portfolios recovered once conditions began improving.

A third category includes financial structures designed to preserve capital while maintaining liquidity under defined conditions. Cash-value insurance structures fall into this category for some investors because they combine capital preservation with accessible borrowing features. During periods when credit markets tighten, access to liquidity can become limited across traditional lending channels. Financial structures that maintain internal liquidity provide a different kind of flexibility during those moments.

The defining feature of these protective assets lies in their behavior rather than their excitement. Assets designed for protection tend to attract less attention during rising markets because their returns often appear modest when compared with rapidly appreciating investments. During strong expansions, investors naturally gravitate toward assets that compound quickly and dominate headlines.

Yet the role of protection becomes clearer during periods of disruption. Assets that seemed quiet during prosperity often provide stability when volatility rises and investor confidence weakens. Their contribution appears in steadiness rather than in dramatic growth, and that steadiness helps preserve flexibility inside the broader financial structure.

This contrast explains why protective assets can feel underwhelming during long periods of expansion while becoming highly valuable during periods of contraction. The same characteristics that limit their growth during booms allow them to maintain stability during stress. Their presence ensures that a portion of the investor's capital remains insulated from the full force of changing market conditions.

Protection therefore functions as more than a defensive layer. A stable reserve of capital changes the investor's ability to respond when the environment shifts, because resilience in one part of the portfolio preserves freedom in another. This dynamic introduces a second role for protection that many investors only recognize during moments of uncertainty.

Protection changes its meaning once it is viewed through the lens of opportunity. A defensive layer preserves capital during stress, and it also preserves choice when others are losing it. That distinction matters because major market declines rarely produce only fear. They also produce mispricing, forced selling, and moments when quality assets become available under conditions that were absent a year earlier. Investors with protected capital can respond to those moments differently because they enter the downturn with room to act.

This is where optionality becomes the real payoff of protection. Optionality means having the freedom to make decisions from strength rather than urgency, especially when market conditions become disorderly. During sharp declines, many people focus on preserving what remains because their structure leaves them few alternatives. Investors with a stable reserve can take a wider view. They are still affected by the environment, though they are less likely to be governed by it.

History repeatedly shows that downturns redistribute assets from the pressured to the prepared. In 2008 and early 2009, households and firms under strain sold homes, equities, and private businesses to meet obligations or reduce uncertainty. Buyers with liquidity and emotional stability entered the same period from a very different position. They were not smarter in some abstract sense. They had protection, and protection gave them the ability to treat fear in the market as a condition to evaluate rather than a command to obey.

This is why some of the best opportunities in finance appear during periods when the public mood is most uncomfortable. Prices fall faster than confidence recovers, and quality often gets sold alongside weakness because markets under stress rarely sort assets carefully in real time. A protected investor can use that gap. The person who has preserved capital during the expansion can re-enter the market during contraction with clearer judgment and better terms.

Protection therefore changes the sequence of action. It allows an investor to spend one part of the cycle defending position and another part of the cycle improving position. That movement from defense back to offense only works when the investor remains stable during the decline, because opportunity belongs to those who still have capital, patience, and access when conditions become difficult. Protection creates the conditions for that shift.

Protection requires a different way of thinking about success. Many people evaluate an investment plan by asking how much it can grow during favorable periods. A more durable approach asks a second question at the same time: how well can it hold together when conditions deteriorate. Growth matters because appreciation builds wealth. Durability matters because preserved wealth remains available for future decisions.

This is where the sequence of the book becomes practical. Income supports cashflow, cashflow supports appreciation, and appreciation eventually requires protection if gains are meant to endure. Once assets have grown, securing a portion of those gains creates a stabilizing layer inside the broader financial structure. Over time that layer changes how the investor experiences volatility, because market stress feels different when every dollar is no longer exposed in the same way.

A protected investor also tends to think more clearly. Calm is rarely treated as a financial asset, though it shapes behavior in every downturn. People with a defensive layer are less likely to confuse a temporary disruption with a permanent collapse, because their structure gives them room to wait and evaluate. Better decisions usually emerge from that room, which is one reason protection belongs to mindset as much as it belongs to asset allocation.

That mindset also explains why protection appears before leverage in the framework. Leverage magnifies outcomes, which makes it powerful and demanding at the same time. In the hands of an unstable investor, leverage can turn volatility into damage because borrowed exposure increases pressure precisely when markets are least cooperative. In the hands of a stable investor, leverage can become a tool for expanding opportunity because the surrounding structure is built to absorb strain.

Protection prepares the ground for that distinction. A defensive layer reduces the chance that leverage will be used from urgency, overconfidence, or financial weakness. It helps ensure that future borrowing decisions are made from a position of stability, where the investor has reserves, perspective, and a clearer sense of timing. This is a structural point more than a moral one. The same financial tool can produce very different outcomes depending on the condition of the system around it.

That is why protection belongs immediately before leverage in the logic of the book. An investor who has learned to preserve gains is in a far better position to expand carefully when conditions justify it. Protection keeps the investor in the game, and leverage determines how much ground can be gained once the foundation is secure.

FREE GIFT: Watch The full CAPL+DR System Training

You just covered a powerful concept. And here's the truth information alone doesn't change your life. Execution does. So I created something for you. I put together a step-by-step video training where I walk you through exactly how to apply everything youjust learned, and take it even further. You can watch it for free. No opt in. No catch. Just scan the QR code or go to https://3twarrioracademy.com/training-capldr

SCAN ME

CHAPTER 14

LEVERAGE

Imagine trying to move a large rock in your backyard. You lean against it with your hands and push with steady effort. The rock shifts a little, then settles back into the soil. Your strength meets resistance, and the limits of your body become clear very quickly.

Now imagine someone walking over with a long metal bar and sliding it under the edge of the rock. They ask you to press down on the other end. The movement looks small, almost unimpressive, yet the rock begins to rise from the ground. Your muscles did not grow stronger during those few seconds. The physics of the situation changed.

For thousands of years, people have relied on that simple tool. It has a short name and a long history.

The lever.

A lever multiplies force. A small push becomes a larger movement when the structure around that push is arranged correctly. The idea fascinated thinkers long before modern finance existed. The Greek mathematician Archimedes once said that with a long enough lever and a place to stand, he could move the world. His point was not about strength. It was about structure.

Financial systems contain their own versions of levers. Most people begin their financial lives relying on effort alone. They work, earn income, save a portion, and slowly build resources over time. Effort and discipline remain important throughout this process. Still, there comes a stage where progress becomes less about pushing harder and more about positioning resources differently. It acts as a structural tool that allows investors to control larger opportunities with less personal capital. The underlying asset does the heavy lifting once the structure is in place. Returns increase more quickly when the asset performs well. Losses also expand more quickly when the asset performs poorly.

This dual effect explains why leverage attracts such mixed reactions. During financial crises it often appears in headlines connected to failure, bankruptcy, and sudden losses. During stable periods it operates quietly in the background of large institutions, real estate portfolios, and investment funds.

The tool itself has remained unchanged through all of those situations. Leverage multiplies outcomes in whichever direction the underlying asset moves. That raises an important question for any investor.

What exactly is being multiplied?

This question explains why leverage appears later in the CAPL framework. Multipliers only become useful once something stable already exists to multiply. A strong structure allows leverage to operate as intended. The presence of leverage alone tells us very little. The foundation beneath it tells us almost everything.

The previous chapter introduced protection as the defensive layer of a financial strategy. Protection creates stability by placing part of a portfolio in assets designed to hold value during uncertain periods. Stability produces something investors rarely notice at first. It creates patience.

Leverage depends heavily on that patience. Borrowed capital introduces fixed obligations that continue regardless of market conditions. Payments arrive on schedule whether an asset performs well or poorly. When stability is missing, those obligations begin to control decisions instead of supporting them.

Three common patterns appear when leverage enters a financial plan too early.

1. Leverage without steady cash flow produces fragility because debt requires consistent payments.
2. Leverage without appreciating assets produces stagnation because borrowed money has little opportunity to grow.
3. Leverage without protection produces panic because downturns can force investors to sell assets during the worst moments.

These patterns appear repeatedly across financial history. The tool remains the same in each case, yet the outcome changes depending on the structure supporting it.

A useful way to understand this sequence is to picture wealth as a building under construction. Cash flow forms the foundation that keeps the structure stable. Appreciation builds the floors where wealth begins to accumulate. Protection surrounds the structure with walls that reduce exposure to storms and unexpected shocks. Leverage functions like an elevator inside that building. It allows movement between levels at a faster pace. When the structure stands on solid ground, the elevator simply improves efficiency. When the structure remains unstable, the elevator increases the speed of collapse.

Many people first encounter leverage long before that structure exists. Student loans appear early in adulthood. Credit cards arrive soon after. Car loans follow. Each of these tools involves borrowed money, yet they operate within a different financial context. In those situations leverage supports consumption rather than investment. Repayment depends almost entirely on future labor. The experience teaches people that debt feels restrictive, stressful, and difficult to control.

Understanding leverage requires separating those experiences from a different category of borrowing. To see the difference clearly, we need to examine the two forms of debt that operate inside modern financial systems.

The Two Faces of Debt

Debt appears in many forms across everyday life. The word itself often carries a sense of pressure because many people first encounter it during ordinary spending decisions. Credit cards, personal loans, and financing plans appear early in adulthood and gradually become part of routine financial behavior.

This form of borrowing connects directly to consumption. A credit card pays for groceries, travel, or household purchases. A personal loan covers a short-term expense or replaces savings during a tight month. Car financing spreads the cost of a vehicle across several years of payments. These transactions feel normal because they are common, yet they share an important feature.

Repayment depends entirely on future labor.

The purchase happens in the present while the work required to repay it stretches into the future. A paycheck becomes the engine that clears the balance over time. When income remains steady, the system works smoothly. When income changes, the obligation remains in place and pressure grows quickly. This pattern creates what we can call survival debt. The debt supports immediate needs or consumption, and repayment requires continuous effort.

Over time, survival debt quietly reduces flexibility because income must first serve obligations created earlier.

Another form of borrowing operates under a different structure. This form connects debt to assets that produce value over time. Rental properties, small businesses, and certain investment structures operate in this way. Borrowed capital enters the picture, yet the asset itself contributes to repayment.

Consider a simple example. A small apartment building generates monthly rent from tenants. A loan helps purchase the property, and the rent collected each month helps service the loan. The investor still carries responsibility, yet the asset participates in the repayment process.

This form of borrowing creates what we can call strategic debt. The structure directs borrowed money toward assets capable of producing income or appreciation. The debt remains present, though the asset itself contributes to carrying the weight.

Both forms involve the same financial tool. The difference appears in intent and structure. Many households borrow against their future work. The wealthy often borrow against assets already producing value. The distinction shapes how leverage influences freedom over time. Once this difference becomes clear, another pattern begins to appear. Borrowing decisions do not only vary by purpose. They also vary by timing. Investors who use leverage carefully tend to introduce it during particular moments in the economic cycle.

Leverage behaves differently depending on the stage of the economic cycle. During long periods of growth, asset prices rise steadily and optimism spreads through markets. Investors see expanding values around them, and borrowing becomes easier to obtain.

Banks increase lending activity. Businesses expand projects using borrowed capital. Households feel comfortable taking on new obligations because recent experience suggests continued growth. The financial system fills with leverage during these expansion phases.

Several conditions appear together during those moments:

- asset prices sit near recent highs
- confidence spreads across markets
- borrowed money becomes widely available

These environments feel safe because the previous years have been favorable. Yet high prices and widespread borrowing reduce the margin for error. Small changes in economic conditions can ripple quickly through a system already carrying significant leverage.

Different conditions appear after disruption. Economic slowdowns, financial crises, or market corrections reduce asset prices and weaken confidence. Investors become cautious, and lenders tighten access to credit. Activity slows while participants evaluate the new landscape.

These moments often produce the opposite set of conditions:

- asset prices fall below previous peaks
- uncertainty replaces confidence
- borrowing becomes less common

Opportunities sometimes appear in these quieter periods because assets trade at lower valuations than before. Recovery phases can produce strong returns as economies stabilize and activity gradually returns. A simple principle often circulates among experienced investors: opportunities during panic require emotional stability. Decisions made in those moments shape long-term outcomes. Leverage often enters the picture at that stage, when patience and preparation meet opportunity. Borrowed capital can amplify recovery when used carefully within a stable structure.

Yet leverage introduces another force that influences every decision made around it.

Emotion.

The Psychology of Leverage

Leverage changes more than financial outcomes. It also changes how people feel while money is at work. A portfolio without debt moves at a pace that allows patience. An investor can watch markets rise and fall while waiting for long-term results to develop. Leverage alters that emotional rhythm because borrowed money introduces obligations that continue regardless of market movement. Payments arrive according to a schedule set months or years earlier. Interest accumulates quietly in the background. The structure places a clock next to every decision.

This clock influences behavior in ways that are often underestimated. Imagine two investors holding the same asset during a temporary market decline. One investor owns the asset outright and can simply wait while conditions improve. The other investor financed part of the purchase with borrowed capital and faces regular loan payments. Both investors may believe in the same long-term outcome. The presence of deadlines changes the emotional experience of the second investor. Time pressure narrows attention and pushes decisions toward immediate relief rather than careful evaluation.

Research in behavioral finance repeatedly shows that pressure influences judgment. People under stress often react faster and with less information. In investing, these reactions sometimes appear as sudden sales, rushed refinancing, or attempts to escape an uncomfortable situation. For this reason, many failures involving leverage begin long before the final outcome becomes visible. The underlying math of the investment may remain sound. The difficulty emerges when emotional pressure alters behavior during uncertain periods.

A useful way to understand this dynamic is to view leverage as a magnifier of personality. Investors who remain calm under pressure often handle leveraged positions with patience and careful planning. Investors who react strongly to uncertainty may find the same structure difficult to manage.

Experienced investors often apply a simple test when evaluating borrowed capital. They ask whether the debt introduces constant worry into their daily lives. Sleep becomes a surprisingly useful indicator. Financial structures that allow calm decision-making tend to remain manageable during volatility.

When debt produces steady anxiety, the structure begins to control the investor rather than support the investment. The distinction becomes visible long before the numbers themselves reveal it. For that reason, investors who use leverage effectively tend to follow a small set of disciplined rules that guide how and when borrowed capital enters their strategy.

Now, borrowed capital increases the scale of opportunity, yet the structure works best when guided by a few simple boundaries. Experienced investors often rely on practical rules that shape how leverage enters their decisions.

The first rule concerns the purpose of the borrowing. Debt connected to consumption gradually reduces flexibility because repayment depends entirely on future labor. Borrowing connected to productive assets follows a different path. Assets capable of generating income or value over time can contribute to the repayment process.

The second rule focuses on cash flow. Loans tied to investments function more smoothly when the underlying asset produces steady income. Rental property offers a familiar example. Tenants pay rent each month, and part of that rent services the mortgage attached to the building. The investor still carries responsibility for the loan, though the asset participates in sustaining the structure.

A third rule addresses flexibility. Healthy leverage leaves room for adjustment when economic conditions change. Loan terms, interest rates, and payment schedules all influence how easily an investor can adapt during uncertain periods. When debt removes flexibility, the structure becomes difficult to manage during normal market fluctuations.

One final rule concerns planning ahead. Every borrowed dollar eventually requires resolution through repayment, refinancing, or asset sale. Investors who introduce leverage thoughtfully consider how that process will unfold before the loan begins. These guidelines shape the difference between leverage as a disciplined tool and leverage as a source of unnecessary pressure. Borrowed capital becomes most effective when it operates inside a stable structure with clear expectations.

The next step involves examining how leverage appears in real financial situations and how investors apply these principles in practice.

Strategic leverage often appears inside financial structures that already serve a protective purpose. Certain assets build value gradually while also providing stability within a broader financial plan. Over time, some of these assets accumulate internal value that can be accessed without selling the asset itself.

Cash value life insurance provides a useful example. Many policies build a reserve of cash value as premiums are paid and the policy matures. That reserve belongs to the policyholder and grows steadily inside the policy. In some cases, the policyholder can borrow against that accumulated value while the policy itself continues operating. This structure creates an interesting dynamic. The underlying asset remains intact and continues building value. At the same time, the borrowed funds provide liquidity that can be directed toward another opportunity. The investor maintains the protective asset while also gaining temporary access to capital.

Consider a simple situation. A policyholder has built substantial value inside a life insurance policy over several years. Instead of withdrawing that value, which would reduce the policy's long-term strength, the policyholder borrows against a portion of it. The borrowed funds might then be used to purchase a rental property or invest in another asset capable of producing income.

The protective layer stays in place while the new investment begins working elsewhere. The structure allows two financial processes to operate at the same time. One continues building stability while the other seeks growth.

For you, this raises an important practical question. How can someone evaluate leverage decisions in a responsible and structured way?

Your Leverage Checklist

Leverage becomes easier to understand when viewed through a series of practical questions. These questions help determine whether borrowed capital supports a stable financial structure or introduces unnecessary pressure.

Step 1 - Confirm the foundation

Before considering leverage, examine the financial base already in place. A stable income stream, appreciating assets, and protective reserves create the conditions where leverage can operate safely. When these elements are missing, borrowed capital often introduces stress rather than opportunity.

Step 2 - Identify productive opportunities

Consider the asset receiving the borrowed capital. Productive assets usually generate income, appreciation, or both over time. Rental property, established businesses, and diversified investments fall into this category. These assets create value that supports the structure surrounding the debt.

Step 3 - Ensure the asset contributes to repayment

Leverage works best when the asset itself participates in servicing the debt. Income generated by the investment can cover part of the loan payments or strengthen the investor's financial position. Structures that rely entirely on wages create additional pressure during uncertain periods.

Step 4 - Stress test the scenario

Responsible investors examine what happens under less favorable conditions. Market values may fall temporarily. Interest rates may change. Income may slow. Considering these scenarios ahead of time helps determine whether the structure can remain stable during unexpected shifts.

Step 5 - Start small

Leverage rarely needs to begin with large commitments. Smaller positions allow investors to understand how borrowed capital behaves inside their financial structure. Experience grows gradually, and adjustments become easier to manage.

These steps reinforce a simple principle. Leverage appears late in a financial journey because it depends on the strength of the structure already in place. When the foundation is prepared, leverage functions as a controlled stage of acceleration within the broader strategy.

Leverage changes the pace of financial progress. Assets that once grew slowly can expand more quickly when borrowed capital amplifies the scale of an investment. Opportunities that once seemed distant begin moving closer within the same economic cycle.

But speed introduces its own challenges. Larger positions increase exposure to market movements, and success can create a sense of momentum that encourages continued expansion. Investors who move through this stage carefully begin to recognize a second responsibility emerging alongside growth.

That responsibility involves protecting the gains created during favorable periods.

Financial history contains many examples of investors who expanded quickly through leverage and later faced difficulty when economic conditions changed. Markets move through cycles that include growth, disruption, recovery, and stabilization. Each stage places different demands on capital and decision making.

Understanding leverage therefore leads naturally to the next discipline. Investors who accelerate growth must eventually decide how to stabilize and protect the wealth that has been created. The transition requires shifting attention from expansion toward preservation. The next chapter explores this discipline in detail. De-risking examines how investors step back after periods of growth, reduce exposure where appropriate, and strengthen the durability of their financial position. Leverage increases the speed of opportunity within the system. De-risking strengthens the freedom that follows from managing that opportunity carefully.

FREE GIFT: Watch The full CAPL+DR System Training

You just covered a powerful concept. And here's the truth information alone doesn't change your life. Execution does. So I created something for you. I put together a step-by-step video training where I walk you through exactly how to apply everything youjust learned, and take it even further. You can watch it for free. No opt in. No catch. Just scan the QR code or go to https://3twarrioracademy.com/training-capldr

SCAN ME

CHAPTER 15

DE-RISKING

A familiar kind of confidence often begins with a screen. You open your retirement account after work and see that the balance has climbed again. The brokerage account looks stronger than it did last year. Your home estimate is higher too. The numbers feel calm and orderly, which makes the future feel calm and orderly as well.

That feeling usually arrives after several good years in a row. Monthly contributions keep going in, markets keep rising, and the account begins to look like proof that the plan is working. A portfolio that was worth $120,000 a few years ago may now show $200,000. A house bought for $350,000 may now look worth $460,000. Progress creates belief because progress feels like confirmation.

This is where the chapter needs to slow down for a moment. The period that feels safest can quietly be the period when risk is growing fastest. Rising prices increase wealth, and they also increase how much of your life depends on those prices staying high. You see a larger balance. The structure underneath it may be changing in a different direction.

Why does that happen?

It happens because markets move in cycles, and cycles change the meaning of success over time. During expansion, earnings improve, credit grows, and investors become more willing to pay higher prices for future growth. During contraction, those expectations tighten, prices adjust, and the same assets that felt stable begin to feel exposed. The pattern is old, and it shows up in every era under different names.

You can see that rhythm in broad economic history. The United States had long stretches of optimism after World War II, during the technology boom of the 1990s, and during the housing run of the early 2000s. Each period made rising asset prices feel normal. Each period also ended by reminding investors that rising prices and lasting safety are separate things. That is a useful distinction because de-risking begins with understanding it clearly.

A sharp example arrived in October 1987. In the five years before that autumn, the Dow Jones Industrial Average had climbed from about 1,000 to more than 2,700. Corporate profits had improved, inflation looked manageable, and investors had good reason to feel encouraged by the direction of the market. The system appeared steady because the recent past had been steady.

Then the market changed much faster than most people expected.

On Monday, October 19, 1987, the Dow fell more than 22 percent in a single day. A portfolio worth $100,000 on Friday could have been worth about $78,000 by Monday evening. That decline still stands as one of the sharpest one-day drops in modern market history. The event became known as Black Monday because the speed of the fall stunned both professionals and households.

The shock mattered because it violated a quiet assumption many investors carried without saying it out loud. People often assume that major market trouble arrives with enough time to think, adjust, and make a plan. Black Monday showed something else. A market can reprice itself in hours when selling pressure spreads across the system at the same time. That possibility changes how you think about safety.

Part of the speed came from market structure. Program trading had become more common, and these computer-driven strategies often triggered sales when prices crossed certain thresholds. As prices fell, more selling was activated. As more selling hit the market, buyers became harder to find at the old prices. Liquidity thinned, which meant lower prices were needed to complete trades.

That process turned decline into acceleration. One sale pushed toward another, and the market began feeding on its own movement. A drop that might have unfolded over weeks under slower conditions was compressed into a single trading session. The mechanism matters because it shows that risk can build inside the plumbing of a market long before the average investor notices it.

Many people who lived through that day described the same strange fact. Their long-term plans had not changed that morning. The companies in their portfolios were still operating. The broad economy had not vanished over the weekend. What changed was the behavior of the market around those assets. The structure moved faster than the story investors were telling themselves.

That distinction is easy to miss, and it is central to this chapter. Risk does not always enter through one reckless decision. It often builds through systems that look stable during calm periods. Thousands of market participants act at once, and their actions can reinforce one another when stress rises. A household investor feels the result at the end of the chain, even though the chain began somewhere else.

This helps explain why market stress feels so personal. The speed of a decline changes the quality of decision-making. A person who felt patient on Friday can feel urgent by Monday because a fast drop changes the emotional weather inside the mind. Long-term thinking becomes harder when the numbers on the screen are falling faster than expected. Time matters because time supports judgment.

Behavioral finance gives this pattern a useful name. People tend to expect the recent past to continue into the future, especially after several years of similar results. Psychologists call this recency bias. The phrase sounds technical, though the experience is ordinary. When markets rise for five straight years, rising begins to feel like the natural state of markets.

That mental habit changes behavior in quiet ways. Investors may let cash reserves shrink because cash looks unproductive during a bull market. They may buy more of the assets that already went up because those assets feel safer after success. They may stop noticing how much of their future is tied to the same set of prices. None of those steps feels dramatic at the time.

Consider a household that began with a balanced investment mix. After a strong run in stocks, that family may discover that equities now make up far more of the total portfolio than intended. The shift happened through appreciation, not through a big new bet. The portfolio looks stronger because the number is larger. The portfolio is also more exposed because more of the family's financial future now depends on one part of the market.

The same thing can happen with real estate. A couple may buy one home in a growing area and then watch prices rise year after year. Encouraged by that success, they may buy a second property because housing has treated them well so far. Their confidence feels earned. Their concentration has also increased, which means their financial life now leans more heavily on one market staying healthy.

This is why risk often peaks near the top of a cycle. Confidence rises with the market, and confidence tends to reduce the feeling that protection is needed. Exposure grows as winning positions become larger. Cash shrinks as it becomes less emotionally appealing. The balance sheet looks stronger on the surface while becoming more sensitive underneath.

A portfolio can become riskier without a single reckless trade. It can become riskier through success itself. When one part of the portfolio keeps winning, it takes up more space. When it takes up more space, more of your future depends on it. That is the quiet arithmetic of exposure. Black Monday makes this lesson vivid because many of the investors caught in that decline had done what they were supposed to do. They had saved, invested, and stayed involved in the market during a long expansion. The problem was not that they had no plan. The problem was that the market shifted faster than their plan had room to absorb. The difference matters because it points directly toward de-risking.

De-risking starts with a simple recognition. Conditions change, and portfolios need to change with them. After strong gains, part of a portfolio can be moved into assets or reserves that make the whole structure steadier. That may mean trimming an oversized position, raising cash, or increasing exposure to assets that behave differently during stress. The goal is to preserve room to think clearly when markets stop cooperating.

De-risking does not mean stepping away from growth. It means preventing growth from quietly turning into fragility. A portfolio can still participate in rising markets while carrying more balance than it did at the peak of optimism. That balance is what gives the investor time, and time is one of the most useful financial assets a person can own.

A person with liquidity and a steadier allocation faces market trouble differently from a person who is fully stretched. The first person can watch, assess, and decide. The second person feels pressure sooner because every decline has larger consequences. The difference shows up in behavior long before it shows up in theory. A strong plan should still function during a hard month.

This is the practical purpose of de-risking. It protects your ability to stay in the game when the cycle turns. It creates distance between market volatility and household decision-making. It keeps a bad week in the market from becoming a bad decision in your life. That is why de-risking belongs after growth in this framework.

The Hidden Risk of Concentration

A portfolio often becomes most fragile while it still looks successful. You check the balance, see years of gains, and feel that the plan is proving itself. One fund has done especially well. One sector keeps leading the market. The larger account feels like greater safety, even when more of that safety now rests on a narrower base.

That is how concentration usually enters a financial life. It rarely arrives through one dramatic decision. It builds through success that keeps repeating in the same place. A position that started as 20 percent of a portfolio can become 35 or 40 percent after several strong years, even when you never meant for it to grow that large.

Portfolios do not grow evenly. Some assets rise faster, attract more attention, and begin taking up more room. The investor sees the gain first. The change in structure comes later, and often quietly. Over time, more of your future depends on one corner of the market continuing to work.

The technology boom of the late 1990s is one of the clearest examples. The internet was spreading quickly through homes, offices, schools, and markets. Companies building software, networking tools, and online businesses seemed tied to a new kind of economic growth. Investors wanted exposure because the story was compelling and the gains were real.

The numbers tell the story clearly. The Nasdaq Composite rose from roughly 750 in 1995 to more than 5,000 by March 2000. That kind of rise changes behavior. Mutual funds increased technology exposure. Pension funds did the same. Individual investors saw friends, neighbors, and coworkers making money in the same part of the market and followed the same path.

The internet story also had real substance, which made the concentration feel even safer. Digital tools did change business, retail, communication, and media. Investors were right about the broad direction of the world. They were less careful about the price they were paying to participate in it. That gap between a true story and a stretched price is where concentration often becomes dangerous.

When a sector rises faster than everything around it, it starts dominating portfolios almost by itself. A balanced account built in 1995 could look very different by 1999 simply because technology holdings had expanded so much. The investor did not need to make a reckless bet. The gains created the imbalance. Success changed the proportions.

That is concentration risk in plain language. A portfolio becomes concentrated when too much depends on one theme, one sector, one region, or one type of asset. You may own many positions and still be concentrated if those positions move for the same reason. A portfolio full of technology names can look diversified on paper while behaving like one large technology bet. By early 2000, this was happening across public markets. Technology stocks had become such a large part of major indexes that broad exposure often meant more technology exposure than investors realized. Some companies traded at prices that assumed years of growth would arrive smoothly and quickly. Earnings did not always support those prices, though confidence in the future did.

Then expectations began to change.

The decline started in March 2000 and deepened over the next two years. The Nasdaq fell from more than 5,000 to near 1,100, a decline of almost 80 percent. Many dot-com firms disappeared because their business models could not survive tighter financial conditions. Even strong companies that later became successful took years to recover in the market.

This is where the lesson becomes useful. The problem was never that technology had no future. The problem was that too much capital had crowded into the same future at the same time. When one story becomes too dominant inside a portfolio, the portfolio becomes less stable even while it appears more rewarding. That is the hidden risk of concentration.

Psychology helps explain why this happens. Strong returns encourage people to believe they understand more than they actually do. A winning investment often feels like proof of insight. If a stock triples, the investor may begin to trust the thesis more deeply and may also trust his own judgment more deeply. That confidence often leads to more exposure rather than more caution. Another force works alongside overconfidence. People love a clean story. A clear narrative helps the mind organize uncertainty into something easier to hold. In the late 1990s, the internet offered exactly that kind of narrative. It was easy to imagine a transformed world, and the market kept rewarding that imagination. The stronger the story became, the easier it was to excuse a portfolio that kept drifting toward one theme.

You can see the same pattern in other markets. A real estate investor may own several properties in one city and feel diversified because the addresses are different. A stock investor may own ten companies linked to artificial intelligence and feel diversified because the tickers are different. A commodity investor may hold several businesses tied to oil demand and feel diversified because the corporate names are different. When the same economic force drives all of them, the portfolio is leaning in one direction.

That is why concentration risk deserves direct language. Different labels do not always create different exposures. If the assets rise for the same reason, they can fall for the same reason. If they depend on the same stream of optimism, they can also suffer from the same turn in sentiment. The portfolio may contain variety in form while remaining narrow in function.

Investors with broader exposure usually fare better when one hot area cools. During the technology collapse, portfolios spread across healthcare, consumer goods, utilities, industrials, and bonds generally held up better than portfolios built around the fastest-growing internet names. The returns during the boom looked less exciting. The structure during the downturn looked far more durable. That difference is the beginning of de-risking.

You do not need to run a pension fund to understand the principle. Imagine a household with most of its investment wealth in one hot sector and very little cash on hand. A sharp market decline now creates two pressures at once. The portfolio is falling in the very place where it is most concentrated, and the household has little flexibility if income is disrupted or a major expense appears. The financial problem is now structural, which means emotion arrives quickly.

Time becomes the missing asset in those moments. A portfolio with adequate liquidity and broader exposure gives you time to think. A portfolio stretched around one dominant theme gives you less time because each market move carries more weight. The difference may look small during a boom. It feels large during a correction.

It protects your ability to choose rather than react. That may mean trimming a position that has become too large, even when that position still looks attractive. It may mean holding a larger cash reserve than the recent market environment seems to justify. It may mean accepting a little less upside in exchange for a structure that can survive a fast change in conditions.

A useful question sits underneath all of this. If prices in your main holdings fell sharply over the next month, would your structure give you room to think clearly? That question reaches farther than market theory. It touches savings, debt, withdrawals, cash needs, and how much of your emotional life is tied to one set of prices. De-risking starts with answering that question honestly.

The answer usually lives in structure, not prediction. You do not need perfect forecasts to reduce concentration. You do not need certainty about interest rates, earnings, or next year's market winner. You need a portfolio that does not depend too heavily on one outcome and a balance sheet that gives you time when prices become unstable. That is a simpler and sturdier standard.

Protecting the Freedom You Built

A financial plan changes once the numbers get large enough to matter in daily life. Early on, growth is the point because small balances need time and market exposure to become meaningful. Later, the question shifts. You begin asking whether the plan can hold together through a hard year, a bad market, or a change in your own life.

That shift happens because money starts carrying more responsibility. A portfolio that once felt like a side project may now sit behind retirement, housing choices, school costs, or work flexibility. A 15 percent decline in a $50,000 account feels very different from the same decline in a $1 million account. The math is the same. The life around the math is different.

Large financial institutions learned this lesson the hard way after the global financial crisis. In 2007 and 2008, many banks relied heavily on short-term funding that looked dependable during calm periods. When confidence weakened, that funding became harder to access. Liquidity dried up quickly, and firms that looked well supplied with assets discovered that assets and usable cash are separate things during stress.

Regulators responded by changing the rules. Under Basel III, banks were required to hold larger amounts of high-quality liquid assets, including instruments that could be turned into cash quickly during a shock. One of the central rules, the Liquidity Coverage Ratio, requires banks to hold enough liquid assets to survive a 30-day stress period. That rule matters because it shows how serious institutions think about survival. They carry buffers before the pressure arrives.

If banks with armies of analysts and central bank support still carry reserves for bad conditions, families and individual investors need reserves too. The scale is different. The principle is the same. A sound financial structure includes room for stress.

That brings us to one of the simplest tools in this chapter: rebalancing. Rebalancing means bringing a portfolio back toward its original design after strong market moves change its shape. It sounds technical. In practice, it is often a quiet correction after success.

Here is what that looks like in ordinary numbers. Imagine you started with 60 percent of your portfolio in stocks and 40 percent in bonds. A strong bull market lifts the stock side much faster than the bond side, and the portfolio drifts to 75 percent stocks and 25 percent bonds. You did nothing reckless. The market made you more exposed by rewarding one part of the portfolio more than the other.

That drift matters because risk can rise without any fresh decision from you. You may still think of yourself as someone with a balanced portfolio. The actual portfolio may now behave like a much more aggressive one. Rebalancing closes that gap by trimming what has grown too large and restoring the mix you meant to own.

The mechanics are simple enough to describe in one sentence: sell some of the asset that grew beyond its target, then move the proceeds into the assets that now make up too little of the portfolio. Many advisors suggest reviewing this once a year or after unusually large moves. The timing matters less than the discipline. The habit is what protects the structure.

The hard part is emotional. Selling part of a winning investment often feels uncomfortable because recent success makes that investment look wise, safe, and full of future promise. A fund that rose 30 percent over the last year feels like the part you should lean into, not reduce. That reaction is understandable because the mind usually trusts what just worked. This is where de-risking becomes psychological as much as financial. You are asking yourself to favor structure over excitement. You are choosing balance over momentum. You are keeping the portfolio aligned with your life rather than with the market's latest mood. That is difficult during a boom because optimism makes excess exposure feel reasonable.

Large institutions do this all the time. Pension funds, endowments, and sovereign wealth funds use target allocations across stocks, bonds, real estate, and private assets. Portfolio managers rebalance because they know a portfolio can drift far from its intended risk level through success alone. They are not trying to guess every market turn. They are protecting the usefulness of the portfolio across many market environments.

You can apply the same logic at home. A family may hold retirement accounts, a brokerage account, home equity, and some cash savings. During a long expansion, stocks may rise faster than everything else, while home values may rise too. The household feels wealthier, which is true. The household may also be relying more heavily on markets and real estate than it realizes. Rebalancing helps bring the financial structure back into proportion.

Consider two retirees who each begin with $1 million and each withdraw $40,000 a year. Over twenty years, both portfolios earn the same 6 percent average annual return. On paper, that sounds like the same result. In life, it can lead to very different outcomes.

Suppose the first retiree gets several poor market years at the start. The portfolio falls while withdrawals are still happening, so each withdrawal removes a larger share of a shrinking base. The math becomes harder because the account has less capital left to recover when markets improve. A bad start leaves a lasting mark.

Now consider the second retiree, who gets stronger returns in the first few years. The account has time to grow before withdrawals take as much weight from it. Later downturns still hurt, though they hurt a larger, more established balance. The same average return leads to a more stable outcome because the sequence arrived in a better order.

This is why de-risking matters so much near retirement, during career changes, or in any period when a portfolio must help fund life directly. The issue is no longer just long-term growth. The issue is whether the portfolio can keep doing its job while markets move through a difficult phase. The order of events begins to matter as much as the events themselves.

Many planners respond to this by building a reserve inside the broader portfolio. That reserve may hold several years of expected living expenses in stable assets or cash-like instruments. When markets fall, those reserves can fund spending without forcing stock sales at depressed prices. When markets recover, the investor can refill the reserve through rebalancing. The structure buys time, and time protects judgment.

Many households today live in a world where wages have grown more slowly than housing, healthcare, and education costs. That means more families depend on investment gains, home equity, and retirement accounts to create long-term stability. Their balance sheets carry more of the burden that wages once carried. That shift changes the cost of a major setback. A household that loses a large portion of its investment assets during a downturn may need years to recover, especially if new savings are limited by rising living costs. The math of recovery gets harder when monthly expenses are already high. A portfolio hit during the wrong season of life can affect work, retirement timing, and family choices all at once.

This is one way wealth concentration deepens over time. Families with diversified portfolios, stronger liquidity, and enough flexibility to avoid forced sales usually stay invested through downturns. Their assets recover when markets recover. Families under tighter pressure may need to sell into weakness to cover living expenses, debt payments, or emergencies. The same market decline produces different long-term outcomes because the structure around the assets is different.

De-risking is not only a portfolio issue. It is also a life issue. A household with some liquidity and a more balanced allocation has more room to make thoughtful decisions. A household stretched around one set of assets, one sector, or one hoped-for outcome has less room because every market swing carries more practical weight.

The goal is to keep your capital useful across different conditions. Growth assets still matter because long-term wealth usually requires ownership in productive things such as businesses, real estate, or other appreciating assets. Stability matters too because growth is only useful if you can hold your position through unstable periods. A plan works best when both functions live inside it. That usually means asking a few steady questions on a recurring basis. Has one part of the portfolio grown too large? Do you have enough liquidity to avoid selling long-term assets during a bad stretch? Has your life changed in a way that should change your allocation? These questions sound modest. Their effect over time is large.

It also means understanding the role of de-risking inside the wider framework of the book. Cashflow creates room. Appreciation grows wealth. Protection secures part of what was built. Leverage can expand opportunity when used with discipline. De-risking makes the whole structure durable enough to survive the next cycle. Each stage supports the next because each stage addresses a different weakness.

This chapter does not ask you to live in fear of downturns. It asks for a portfolio and a household structure that can live through them without losing coherence. That is a calmer and more useful standard. Markets will continue to rise and fall. Interest rates will continue to shift. Economic cycles will continue to test people at uneven moments in life.

Your advantage does not come from predicting each turn. It comes from being prepared for the fact that turns keep coming. Rebalancing, liquidity reserves, and thoughtful allocation sound plain compared with exciting market stories. Plain tools often carry the greatest weight during periods of pressure because they keep a financial life from becoming overly dependent on one outcome.

That is the deeper purpose of protecting the freedom you built. Freedom in finance means having choices when conditions become difficult. It means a rough market does not immediately force a change in your work, your home, or your long-term plan. It means your assets support your life with enough stability that short-term volatility stays in its proper place.

A durable financial life usually looks quieter than people expect. It includes assets that grow, reserves that wait, and a structure that can handle a season of stress without coming apart. That kind of stability does not attract much attention during a boom. It becomes very valuable during everything that follows. That is why de-risking belongs at this stage of the journey.

CHAPTER 16

WISDOM - MASTERING THE CYCLE

Every generation eventually discovers the same uncomfortable truth.

Money moves in cycles. Not the neat cycles that economists draw on charts, or the tidy expansions and contractions described in textbooks. The real cycles feel messier. They appear slowly, disguise themselves as progress, then turn abruptly enough to make the past look obvious in hindsight.

For most people, the pattern becomes visible only after they have already lived through it.

The excitement arrives first. Opportunity spreads through conversation and headlines. Prices rise in ways that feel almost natural, as if the world has discovered a new gear that will keep turning indefinitely. People begin to feel clever simply for participating. Confidence expands quietly, reinforced by results that seem to confirm every decision.

Then the environment shifts. Sometimes the shift arrives suddenly, like a storm breaking over a calm afternoon. Other times it arrives gradually, through small disappointments that accumulate until the story people believed no longer holds together. The result is the same. What once looked inevitable begins to look fragile.

Those who entered the cycle late feel the damage first. Those who borrowed heavily feel it next. Those who assumed the environment would remain stable feel it last. And by the time the pattern becomes obvious, the opportunity has already moved somewhere else. The strange thing about cycles is that they rarely surprise history. They surprise participants.

People living inside the boom almost never believe they are inside one.

Winning creates a powerful illusion. When something works once, the mind naturally assumes the same approach will work again. Success feels like confirmation. It suggests that the world operates according to rules we have finally understood.

For a brief period, this belief feels justified. During the technology surge of the late 1990s, countless new investors entered the stock market for the first time. Internet companies appeared almost daily. Valuations climbed at a pace that seemed to reward anyone willing to participate. Stories of sudden wealth circulated through offices, universities, and dinner tables.

A young engineer in California once described that period with surprising honesty. He invested modest savings into a handful of technology stocks and watched his portfolio triple within months. Friends began asking for advice. Confidence followed quickly.

The engineer believed he had developed a talent for spotting the future. Then the cycle turned.

Within two years, most of those companies vanished. The engineer eventually rebuilt his savings through steady work and cautious investing, yet he would later admit that the most valuable lesson from that experience had nothing to do with technology.

It had everything to do with timing. The market had rewarded participation, not foresight. This distinction matters more than most people realize. Success often teaches the wrong lesson.

Human behavior rarely changes as quickly as technology does. Markets evolve. Financial tools become more sophisticated. Entire industries rise and fall within decades. Yet the emotional patterns that guide decision making remain stubbornly familiar. Excitement spreads easily. Confidence grows in environments where recent outcomes look favorable. When people observe others succeeding, they naturally assume the opportunity remains available.

This dynamic fuels nearly every economic boom.

At first the enthusiasm appears rational. New ideas attract investment because they promise improvement. Early adopters benefit from the growth that follows. Over time, however, participation expands beyond understanding.

People begin to invest in things they barely recognize because others appear to be prospering. Stories replace analysis. Momentum replaces caution. Eventually the distance between expectation and reality becomes too large to ignore.

The cycle corrects itself.

What disappears during that correction is rarely the idea itself. What disappears is the excess confidence that accumulated around it. The same pattern repeats because the same emotions guide it. Optimism during the rise. Fear during the fall.

Memory fades between the two.

Many people believe financial success depends primarily on information. They study markets. They analyze companies. They search for signals that reveal where the next opportunity might appear. Knowledge becomes a tool for navigating uncertainty.

Knowledge certainly helps. Yet the most difficult decisions rarely involve information. They involve restraint. Anyone can recognize an opportunity when enthusiasm surrounds it. The environment itself provides encouragement. Prices move upward. Headlines reinforce the narrative. Friends begin to participate.

The harder question appears later.

When should enthusiasm be treated with caution?

Wisdom develops slowly through experience with these moments. It recognizes that environments change even when the underlying story remains attractive. It understands that timing influences outcomes as strongly as analysis.

- An investor with knowledge might ask what to buy.
- An investor with wisdom begins by asking when.

Markets reveal a simple truth about human psychology. People feel safest moving with the crowd. When everyone around us behaves the same way, uncertainty appears smaller. Shared belief reduces the discomfort of risk because the responsibility feels distributed. If the outcome turns negative, at least we were not alone.

This instinct explains much of the behavior that drives cycles.

During periods of expansion, the crowd grows confident together. The presence of many participants creates the impression of stability. Prices rise because participation rises, reinforcing the belief that participation itself is correct.

The same process occurs during decline. Fear spreads through headlines and conversation. Investors sell because others are selling. Each decision appears individually rational while the collective outcome amplifies the decline.

The crowd rarely intends to create instability. It simply reacts. Those who maintain emotional discipline during these periods behave differently. They observe the same environment without allowing it to dictate their actions. This requires patience that often feels uncomfortable, especially when the crowd appears certain.

Yet history shows that calm behavior during moments of collective emotion often creates the greatest advantage.

People who endure across multiple cycles begin to notice something that newcomers rarely see.

Time changes the meaning of success. A single year of extraordinary gains attracts attention. It creates stories that circulate widely because they feel dramatic and immediate. Yet those stories rarely include what happens afterward.

Long-term investors view success through a different lens. They measure results across decades rather than seasons. They recognize that periods of rapid growth usually alternate with periods of adjustment. Their goal becomes continuity rather than excitement.

This perspective alters behavior in subtle ways. Risk becomes something to manage rather than chase. Opportunities are evaluated according to durability rather than novelty. Losses become temporary setbacks instead of permanent failures. The result often appears quiet from the outside. There are fewer dramatic victories and fewer catastrophic mistakes.

Over time, however, this quiet approach accumulates surprising strength.

Early in life, wealth often represents possibility. It promises freedom from constraint, the ability to choose work, location, or lifestyle without constant financial pressure. Accumulation becomes the primary goal because it expands the range of options available.

As years pass, the meaning of wealth begins to shift. Security becomes more important than acceleration. People begin to think about stability for their families, protection against unexpected events, and the long-term preservation of what they have already built.

Eventually another layer appears. Responsibility. Wealth creates influence whether its owner intends it or not. Decisions about spending, investing, and inheritance shape opportunities for others long after the original effort has ended. Families who maintain wealth across generations often recognize this shift early. They begin to treat wealth as something that requires stewardship rather than constant expansion. Systems replace improvisation. Patience replaces urgency.

This transition reflects a deeper form of wisdom. The purpose of wealth evolves with time.

The people who master cycles rarely appear extraordinary while the cycle unfolds. During booms they may seem cautious. During declines they may seem patient to a fault. Their decisions attract little attention because they lack the drama that headlines prefer.

Yet over long periods their position strengthens. They avoid the excess risk that destroys portfolios during downturns. They maintain enough flexibility to act when opportunities reappear. Their progress feels steady rather than explosive.

Eventually the difference becomes visible. The investor who endured quietly owns assets that once belonged to those who reacted emotionally. This transfer rarely feels dramatic in the moment. It unfolds through years of discipline and restraint. By the time the pattern becomes obvious, the advantage is already established.

Understanding cycles changes the way people approach wealth. It encourages patience. It reduces the temptation to chase sudden opportunity. It emphasizes preparation over prediction.

Yet one question remains.

What is the purpose behind all of it?

Accumulating resources without direction eventually loses meaning. Security alone cannot define a life. Wealth creates possibilities that extend beyond personal comfort, possibilities that involve influence, responsibility, and legacy.

At some point the focus shifts from building wealth to understanding what wealth should serve. This transition marks the final stage of financial sovereignty. Because surviving the cycle is only part of the journey. The deeper question concerns what you choose to build once you understand how the system truly works.

The next chapter explores that question. And the answer changes everything.

CHAPTER 17

FINANCIAL SOVEREIGNTY - BECOMING THE GENERATIONAL SHIFTER

Once you see how the system works, a strange feeling begins to settle in.

At first the feeling resembles frustration. Many people spend years believing they misunderstood money or failed to work hard enough. They assume the discomfort they feel around finances comes from personal mistakes. When the larger structure becomes visible, the story changes. The problem was never effort alone. The problem was the environment that effort had to operate inside.

This realization can feel unsettling because it removes a familiar explanation. For years the middle class story offered a clear path. Study carefully. Work steadily. Save consistently. The reward would arrive later in the form of stability and security. That promise shaped life decisions across several generations. Families organized their expectations around it.

When that promise weakens, people search for explanations close to home. They work longer hours. They collect more qualifications. They reduce spending and delay major life decisions. Each adjustment feels responsible. Each adjustment also quietly assumes the system still functions the way it once did.

The discomfort many people feel today comes from a simple misalignment. The instructions remained stable while the environment continued changing. Behaviors that once protected families now struggle to produce the same results. People follow the path faithfully and arrive somewhere different from where they expected.

Once that misalignment becomes clear, a different question begins to appear.

What happens when the rules you inherited no longer match the world you live in?

Most people respond to that question with hesitation. The old rules still carry emotional weight because they came from people who cared deeply about security. Parents and grandparents passed down habits that helped them survive uncertainty. Those habits were rooted in real experience. Questioning them can feel like rejecting the wisdom of the people who raised you.

Understanding the origin of those behaviors makes the situation easier to interpret. Your grandparents experienced an economic collapse that erased savings and jobs with little warning. Stability became the highest priority because instability had already shown its consequences. Institutions that promised continuity offered relief from fear. Trusting those systems made sense in that moment.

The world that followed rewarded those instincts for several decades. Stable employment produced rising wages. Home ownership created predictable wealth. Pensions promised retirement security without requiring complex financial decisions. The system functioned well enough to justify loyalty.

Over time those conditions changed quietly. Global competition increased. Debt expanded. Institutions that once carried risk on behalf of workers slowly shifted that responsibility back onto individuals. Retirement planning moved from guaranteed pensions to personal accounts. Job security weakened while housing and education became more expensive.

The structure remained recognizable even as its guarantees faded.

This is where confusion begins. People continue behaving as though the system still provides the same protections. They save cash believing it preserves value. They remain loyal to employers expecting stability. They assume retirement will eventually take care of itself. These behaviors once made sense because the environment supported them.

Today the environment asks for something different. Recognizing this shift does not require rejecting the past. It requires understanding the difference between inherited behavior and present conditions. Your grandparents followed rules designed for their world. You live in a different one.

The moment that difference becomes visible, a new responsibility appears.

Someone must adapt first. Every family history eventually reaches a point where inherited habits stop producing the outcomes they once did. At that moment one person begins to notice the pattern. That person studies the system more closely. They begin asking questions that previous generations never needed to ask.

This individual becomes the generational shifter. The title sounds dramatic, yet the role itself is quiet. A generational shifter rarely announces their intentions. They simply begin approaching money differently. They read more carefully. They think about ownership rather than only income. They observe how economic systems move over long periods of time.

These behaviors look ordinary from the outside. Their consequences appear slowly.

Consider a simple example.

A young engineer begins investing a small percentage of income each month instead of leaving savings entirely in cash. At first the difference feels minor. The account grows gradually while daily life continues unchanged. Ten years later the investments have produced more wealth than the original savings could have generated alone. Nothing dramatic happened in a single moment. The shift occurred because one person decided to understand how the system actually worked.

Small adjustments compound over time in ways that are difficult to notice at first. The first generation learns the system. The second generation grows up inside a household that understands it. By the third generation the habits feel natural.

This is how financial trajectories change.

The process rarely feels revolutionary while it unfolds. It often begins with curiosity rather than ambition. Someone notices that money behaves differently than they were taught. They begin reading about inflation, investing, and ownership. They experiment with small decisions that gradually reshape their financial structure.

Each step produces slightly more independence. Independence in this context means something specific. It means having the ability to respond when circumstances change. A household with savings can absorb temporary setbacks. A household with assets can generate income outside traditional employment. A household that understands financial systems can adapt strategies as conditions evolve.

This condition is often called financial sovereignty. Sovereignty does not require isolation from the economy. People with financial sovereignty still participate in the same markets and institutions as everyone else. The difference appears in the number of choices available when pressure arrives.

Choice becomes the quiet measure of freedom. A person with one paycheck and no savings has very little room to respond when that paycheck disappears. A person with multiple income streams and accumulated assets has more time to think carefully before acting. Time changes the quality of decisions.

Many of you encounter this idea and immediately assume sovereignty requires extraordinary wealth. That assumption grows from the way financial success is often portrayed in media and culture. Wealth appears as something sudden, dramatic, and distant from ordinary life.

In practice, sovereignty develops slowly through structure.

A household that spends slightly less than it earns begins accumulating savings. Savings create the first layer of resilience. Investments convert savings into assets that grow over time. Ownership gradually produces income that no longer depends entirely on labor.

None of these steps require sudden transformation. They require patience and attention.

Consider a family that saves five percent of its income each year. The amount feels small during the first few years. The savings account grows slowly while daily responsibilities continue demanding attention. After ten years the accumulated capital begins creating options that did not previously exist.

The process continues quietly. The goal is not perfection. Economic cycles rise and fall, and mistakes occur along the way. Sovereignty grows from the ability to adjust rather than from the ability to predict everything correctly. Flexibility matters more than certainty.

This perspective changes how financial decisions feel. Instead of chasing perfect timing, people focus on building durable structures. They prioritize assets that hold value across long periods of time. They maintain liquidity that allows patience when markets fluctuate. They treat knowledge about economic systems as a lifelong habit rather than a temporary project.

The result is a gradual shift in posture.

Fear becomes less dominant because options expand. Decisions become calmer because time pressure decreases. Money stops functioning only as a source of anxiety and begins functioning as a tool for stability. This shift also changes the environment within a household. Children who grow up watching thoughtful financial decisions develop a different relationship with money. Conversations about saving, investing, and ownership happen openly rather than quietly. Financial awareness becomes normal rather than mysterious.

Over time the family culture evolves.

What began as curiosity in one generation becomes common sense in the next. Behaviors that once required deliberate effort become routine. Financial sovereignty moves from individual practice into shared identity. This is why the idea of the generational shifter matters. The person who begins this process rarely receives recognition in the moment. Their work unfolds slowly and often privately. They study systems others ignore. They practice habits that feel unfamiliar to the people around them.

Years later the results become visible. Children grow up in households where money is understood rather than feared. Financial decisions happen with clarity instead of confusion. Opportunities appear that previous generations never had access to.

The shift becomes part of the family story. Looking back, the change rarely appears dramatic. It often begins with one simple decision. Someone chooses to understand the system instead of assuming it will take care of them. That decision marks the beginning of sovereignty.

Not because it guarantees success, but because it changes the relationship between individuals and the structures around them. People who understand the system move through it with greater awareness. They recognize risks earlier. They notice opportunities others overlook.

Over time this awareness compounds just like financial capital.

The middle class system once offered stability by absorbing uncertainty on behalf of individuals. That arrangement functioned for several decades because the environment supported it. As conditions changed, the responsibility for navigating uncertainty slowly returned to households.

This shift can feel overwhelming when it appears suddenly.

Yet it also restores something older.

Before the middle class existed as a structured promise, families maintained security through ownership, skill, and adaptability. They built resilience directly rather than outsourcing it to institutions. The world today does not require returning to that earlier era. It does, however, reward many of the same instincts.

- Understanding systems.
- Maintaining flexibility.
- Building assets that endure.

These behaviors form the foundation of financial sovereignty. When you recognize this pattern, the purpose of the journey becomes clearer. The goal was never simply wealth. Wealth can appear and disappear depending on the environment surrounding it.

The deeper goal is independence of judgment.

People who understand how financial systems work are less likely to be surprised by their movements. They approach decisions with context rather than assumption. They recognize the difference between temporary comfort and lasting security. This awareness changes the trajectory of a life.

More importantly, it changes the trajectory of a family. Somewhere in every family history there is a moment when someone begins seeing the system clearly for the first time. That moment often arrives quietly. It begins with curiosity and develops through consistent learning.

From that point forward the path begins to shift.

You may already be standing inside that moment.

Understanding how the system works does not require abandoning everything that came before. It simply invites you to move through the world with clearer eyes. The rules you inherited came from people who adapted to their environment. You now have the same responsibility within yours.

This is how generational change begins.

Not through sudden revolutions, but through steady awareness.

And awareness, once it appears, rarely disappears again.

FREE GIFT: Watch The full CAPL+DR System Training

You just covered a powerful concept. And here's the truth information alone doesn't change your life. Execution does. So I created something for you. I put together a step-by-step video training where I walk you through exactly how to apply everything youjust learned, and take it even further. You can watch it for free. No opt in. No catch. Just scan the QR code or go to https://3twarrioracademy.com/training-capldr

SCAN ME

FINAL CHAPTER

THE CHOICE THAT REMAINS

By the time you reach the end of this book, the system may look different than it did when you began. At the start, many people sense that something about money feels increasingly fragile. They work harder than previous generations seemed to need to. They earn more credentials, carry more responsibility, and plan carefully for the future. Yet stability often feels temporary, as if it could shift without warning. The effort is real, but the ground beneath it feels less certain.

That feeling is not imaginary. Over the previous chapters, we traced the structure that produced it. The middle class was never simply the natural result of effort. It emerged from a particular moment in history, shaped by fear, policy, and economic conditions that favored stability over volatility. For several decades the arrangement worked well enough to appear permanent.

But permanence was never guaranteed. As the environment changed, the rules stayed largely the same. Behaviors that once protected families slowly lost their effectiveness. Saving cash preserved wealth in one era and quietly reduced it in another. Loyalty to institutions once produced security and later produced dependency. The instructions remained visible even as the environment evolved.

Many people feel this shift without fully understanding its cause. They assume the problem lies in personal discipline or effort. They blame themselves for outcomes that seem increasingly difficult to control. Yet when the larger structure becomes visible, the story begins to look different. The discomfort so many people feel today often reflects a system that has changed faster than the behaviors built to operate inside it.

Seeing that clearly can be unsettling. It removes a familiar explanation and replaces it with responsibility. Once the system becomes visible, it becomes difficult to move through it blindly again. You begin noticing how money flows, how incentives shape decisions, and how institutions distribute risk. Patterns that once felt random begin to reveal structure.

This awareness does not immediately solve every problem. It does something more important. It restores agency.

For most of my life, I did not see the system clearly either. I followed the same assumptions that many people inherit. Work hard. Build something stable. Trust that effort would translate into security. Those beliefs shaped my early path as an entrepreneur and business owner.

Then the pandemic arrived. Businesses closed across the country almost overnight. Revenue disappeared with a speed that no business plan had prepared for. Many entrepreneurs experienced the same shock during that period. Years of work could be disrupted by forces completely outside individual control.

In moments like that, two things become very clear.

The first is how fragile many structures actually are. Systems that appear stable for years can change suddenly when conditions shift. Institutions protect themselves first. Markets adjust without warning. Plans built for one environment struggle to survive in another.

The second realization arrives more quietly.

What matters most is not what you lose. It is what remains. When my businesses collapsed during that period, I lost income, stability, and the structures that had previously supported my life. What I did not lose was the ability to learn. I did not lose the discipline required to rebuild. I did not lose the willingness to study the system more deeply than I had before.

That shift changed everything. Instead of trying to outrun the system or complain about its unfairness, I began studying how it actually worked. I read the thinkers who had spent decades examining economic cycles, investment behavior, and the structure of money itself.

Some of those voices will be familiar to many readers.

Ray Dalio wrote extensively about the long arc of economic empires and monetary systems. Warren Buffett and Charlie Munger demonstrated the power of disciplined ownership over long periods of time. Robert Kiyosaki reframed the relationship between labor and assets in ways that forced many people to reconsider how income truly functions.

Books that explored these ideas began reshaping how I understood the environment around me.

- The Changing World Order
- Cashflow Quadrant
- Think and Grow Rich
- The Intelligent Investor
- The Richest Man in Babylon

Each approached money from a slightly different perspective, yet they shared a common theme. Financial systems reward understanding more than effort alone. Those who learn how capital moves can position themselves differently from those who simply participate without awareness.

Knowledge, however, rarely changes outcomes by itself. Many people read excellent books and continue living the same financial life they lived before. Information accumulates without transforming behavior. The difference appears when knowledge becomes structure.

Over time I began building a framework that organized what I was learning. It did not appear all at once. It developed through experimentation, mistakes, and careful observation of how money actually moved through the modern economy.

Eventually that structure became what I now call CAPL + DR and what we have discussed over the course of the book. The details of that framework matter less than the principle behind it. Systems create consistency where motivation cannot. Motivation rises and falls depending on circumstances and emotion. Systems continue operating even when enthusiasm fades.

When the system is clear, action becomes easier. This realization returns us to the idea that runs quietly through the entire book. Every generation inherits a set of assumptions about money, work, and security. Those assumptions reflect the environment that shaped the generation before them. When the environment changes, the assumptions require adjustment.

Someone has to recognize that shift first.

The first generation learns the system. The second generation grows up inside a household that understands it. By the third generation the habits feel natural. This is how trajectories change. No system removes uncertainty completely. Economic cycles will continue rising and falling. Markets will continue shifting as technology and policy evolve. The goal has never been perfect control over those forces.

The goal is sovereignty.

Once that possibility becomes visible, the final step belongs entirely to you Many people will finish a book like this with curiosity and then return to the habits they already know. Life is busy, and familiar routines require less effort than unfamiliar ones. Knowledge can sit quietly on a shelf for many years without changing anything.

Others will do something different. They will begin observing the system around them more carefully. They will test small adjustments in how they save, invest, and think about ownership. Over time those adjustments will grow into structures that support a different financial future.

The difference between those two outcomes does not lie in intelligence or opportunity.

It lies in a single decision.

Whether the awareness gained here becomes action. If you have read this far, you have already taken the first step. You chose to examine the system rather than assume it would always work the way it once did. That willingness to look deeper is rare enough on its own.

Where that curiosity leads from here is entirely yours to decide. The system will continue evolving regardless of what any individual chooses. Economic cycles will move forward, institutions will adapt, and new generations will inherit the results. What remains constant is the opportunity each person has to understand the environment they live inside.

And once that understanding arrives, the path forward becomes clearer. The responsibility no longer belongs to the system. It belongs to you.

Welcome to the future of our monetary system. A future that is bright. A future that is hopeful. A future your family will be proud you helped create. You chose sovereignty. You chose responsibility. You chose freedom.

God bless you. And remember - God is good, all the time.

With love and respect,
Coach JV

OUR NEXT STEP STARTS NOW

You've reached the end of this book... now it's time to apply it.

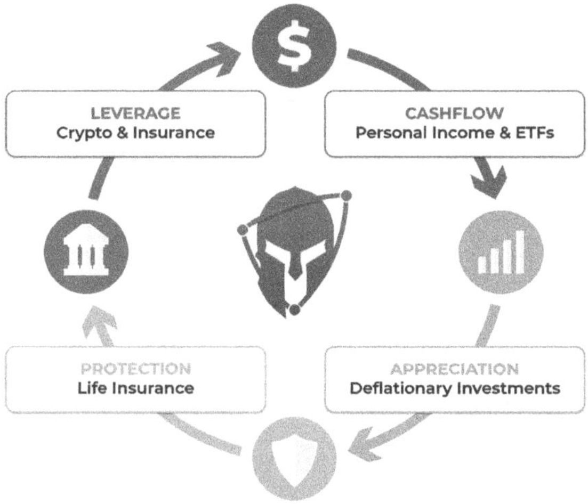

This step-by-step video training shows you exactly how to implement everything you've learned and take it further.

SCAN TO START THE TRAINING

YOU CAN WATCH IT FOR FREE. NO OPT-IN. NO CATCH

https://3twarrioracademy.com/training-capldr

www.ingramcontent.com/pod-product-compliance
Lightning Source LLC
LaVergne TN
LVHW022213200926
848481LV00006B/1956
9798995775201